WOODY PLANTS
of the SOUTHWEST

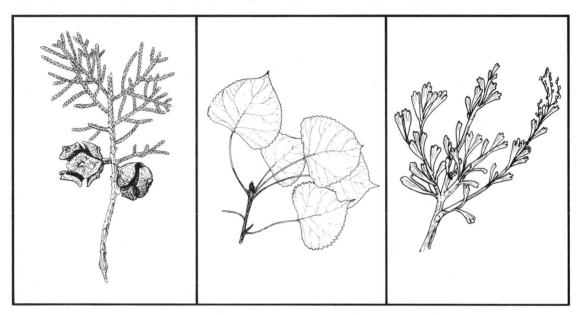

A FIELD GUIDE WITH DESCRIPTIVE TEXT, DRAWINGS, RANGE MAPS AND PHOTOGRAPHS

Samuel H. Lamb

SUNSTONE
PRESS

SANTA FE

Dedicated to the memory of Minnie Solomon Lamb who spent many hours alongside the road, without complaint, as I gathered plants, wood specimens, and took pictures.

Drawings by Norma Ames

All photographs are by the author with the following exceptions: **Orville Freeman,** p. 30 (both); p. 71 (Indigo bush); p. 84 (Joshua tree); p. 114 **Roy Barker**, cover, p.4, p. 150 (Yellow trumpet).

Printed in the United States of America

10 9 8 7 6 5

Library of Congress Cataloging in Publication Data:
Lamb, Samuel H. 1909-
    Woody Plants of the Southwest.
1. Woody Plants—Southwest, New—Indetification.
    I. Title.
QK484.S89L35   582'.15'0979   76-357696
ISBN: 0-913270-50-4

Published by SUNSTONE PRESS
                Post Office Box 2321
                Santa Fe, NM 87504-2321 / USA
                (505) 988-4418 / *orders only* (800) 243-5644
                FAX (505) 988-1025

CONTENTS

INTRODUCTION

AND

ACKNOWLEDGEMENTS

Much of the material used in this book was first prepared for Bulletin Number 14 of the New Mexico Department of Game and Fish under the title *Woody Plants of New Mexico and Their Value to Wildlife*. Under agreement with that department, the material has been used here, but the ranges have been extended to cover not only New Mexico but southern Colorado, southern Utah, southern Nevada, southeastern California, and all of Arizona. Northern Mexico and western Texas are also often included.

Also, the number of species of plants included was greatly expanded to cover the plants that occur outside New Mexico. Some corrections have been made where further research has shown the material in the original publication to have been in error.

The author has gathered wood from all the species usually considered to be trees in New Mexico and also from all the shrubs that normally produce stems more than an inch in diameter. Several additions were made to this collection from Arizona and southern California insofar as the laws would permit. From these collections descriptive notes concerning the wood have been added to the plant descriptions. The color of the wood is frequently helpful in identifying the plant.

Information on derivation of scientific names has been included to help in tying the scientific name to the plant. Sources have included Vines, Little, Featherly, and others.

All but a few of the pictures were taken by the author. Others have been supplied by Orville Freeman and Roy Barker. The drawings of plant detail have been done by Mrs. Norma Ames. Her daughter, Karen Ames, did the art work on the maps.

The descriptions of the plants are limited largely to the gross characteristics that will be readily observable in the field. Detailed floristic descriptions would have been unduly long and are well covered in standard botanical works, which are available to the scientist requiring complete detail.

The distribution maps suggest the area where the various trees and shrubs occur and are too small to give detail. Many species have even more limited distribution within the area shown as their range. For example, the tops of the desert mountains will provide suitable habitat for species of trees and shrubs found in the mountains farther north. The topography of our area is so broken that it is very difficult to indicate detailed distribution, even when large maps are used. Many of the standard books on the flora of the Southwest give distribution only by counties, but even this is misleading, as one county may have terrain representative of the desert, the mesas, and the high mountains. However, we considered the small maps useful in alerting the reader to the areas of likely occurrence of the plants.

A study of the distribution maps will show that many of the species found in southern New Mexico also extend into Chihuahua, Mexico, and those in southern Arizona overlap into Sonora, Mexico. Thus the value of the book does not stop at the border. Mexican names have been supplied for the plants where it was felt that reasonably reliable names were available. (Mexican names appear within quotation marks.) This, combined with the Latin names that are universal, will make the book of value even to one who does not read the English text. Authority for the Mexican names is from *Meet Flora Mexicana* by M. Walter Pesman, *Trees and Shrubs of Mexico* by Paul C. Standley, and *Timbers of the New World* by Samuel J. Record and Robert W. Hess.

ALLTHORN FAMILY
(Koeberliniaceae)

Allthorn or crucifixion-thorn
"Corona de Cristo"
Koeberlinia spinosa

The genus name honors C.L. Koeberlin, a German clergyman, and *spinosa* refers to the abundant thorns. In fact, the plant usually looks as if it were nothing but thorns.

The plant is generally found in a leafless condition but has small leaves for a part of the season. The small, greenish-white flowers are borne in small clusters on the twigs, and later the small, black fruits will be found attached to the twigs with a short, hairlike stem. The fruits are only about ¼ inch in diameter. The stems are stiff and stout. They fork and refork until they are tangled. The bark is dark green on the younger twigs and gray to dark brown on older older ones. The plant is seldom over about 5 feet tall in our area, and the stems may be up to about 5 inches in diameter. The sapwood is straw-colored and the heart is streaked light and dark brown. The wood is heavy, hard and dense.

This plant has little value to wildlife, except as nesting sites for desert song birds or escape cover for quail.

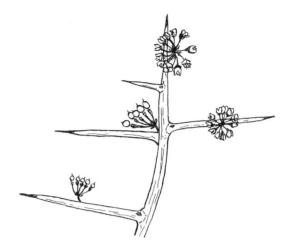

crucifixion–thorn

crucifixion thorn

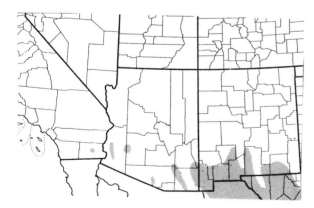

crucifixion--thorn

crucifixion thorn (detail)

2

AMARYLLIS FAMILY
(Amaryllidaceae)

Palmer agave—*Agave palmeri*
Parry agave—*Agave parryi*
Lechuguilla—*Agave lechuguilla*
"Lechuguilla"
Utah agave—*Agave utahensis*
New Mexico agave—*Agave neomexicana*
Golden flowered agave—*Agave palmeri* var.
    chrysantha

    Agave is from the Greek word *agaue* which means noble. *Palmeri* and *parryi* each honor men; *utahensis* and *neomexicana* are named for States; *lechuguilla* is from a Mexican word for little lettuce; *chrysantha* refers to yellow.

    It is a little difficult to think of agaves, or century plants as they are popularly called, as shrubs. However, they are so conspicuous over their range that they should be given some coverage in any book on Southwestern plants.

    Palmer agave will be found in southeast Arizona and southwest New Mexico. Parry agave is much more widely spread through central and southeastern Arizona and across southern New Mexico. Lechuguilla occurs in west Texas and southern New Mexico, south deep into Mexico. Utah agave is found in southwestern Utah and in the region of the Grand Canyon in Arizona. New Mexico agave is limited to south-central and southeastern New Mexico, and golden-flowered agave occurs in the same general areas as Palmer agave.

    The agave plant consists of a rosette of long, slender, thick and leathery leaves that send up a tall flower stalk, ripen seeds, and then die. The leaves may be as small as 1 inch wide and 6 inches long in the smallest one, to 60 to 80 inches long and up to 9 inches wide in the common century plant. Ours all fall between these limits. The agaves occur on rocky slopes and hillsides in the desert foothills.

    Yuccas resemble agaves superficially but do not die following flowering. Also, several species of yucca develop trunks, whereas agaves do not.

Parry agave

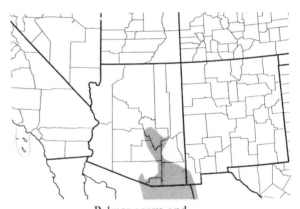

Palmer agave and
Golden-flowered agave

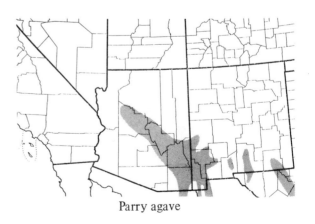

Parry agave

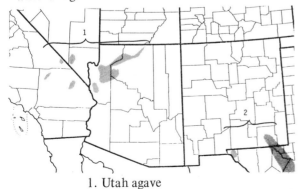

1. Utah agave
2. New Mexico agave

3

ASH FAMILY
(*Oleaceae*)

New Mexico olive—*Forestiera neomexicana*
Desert-olive forestiera—*F. phillyreoides*

The genus name honors a French physician, Charles Le Forestier. *Phillyreoides* means resembling *phillyrea*, a related European genus.

New Mexico olive is a clump-forming shrub 6 to 10 feet tall. It generally occurs in the moister sites at the bases of cliffs or in creek or river bottoms. The simple opposite leaves are narrow and grayish-green in color. The flowers, borne in axils of the leaves, are inconspicuous. The small, black fruits ripen in summer and are very bitter, but relished by song birds. The shrub is not considered valuable to game except as cover, but has shown up in deer diets in three mountain ranges. The wood is white, very hard and heavy, and the grain is somewhat curly. Because of these characteristics it is listed in the dictionary as ironwood, a common name used for any very hard wood. The wood is not large enough for commercial use. The shrub is widely scattered in our area, occurring in southern California, eastward through southern Utah, southwestern Colorado, in Arizona above the desert, and in the western two-thirds of New Mexico to western Texas.

Desert-olive forestiera is very similar to New Mexico olive except that the leaves may be a little longer, not toothed but with the edges rolled under. Its distribution is limited to a few mountains from near Tucson westward through the southern part of Arizona.

Parry agave

New Mexico olive

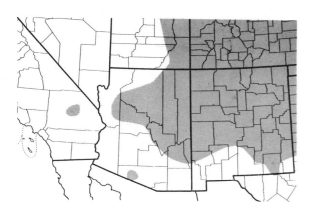

New Mexico olive

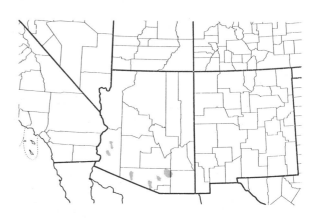

desert olive

4

ASH FAMILY
(Oleaceae)

Singleleaf ash—*Fraxinus anomala*
Lowell ash—*F. lowellii*
Fragrant ash—*F. cuspidata*
"Fresno"
Gregg ash—*F. greggii*
"Barreta china"
Velvet ash—*F. velutina*
"Fresno"

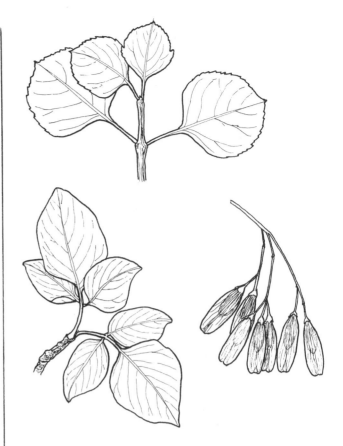

Fraxinus is the classical Latin name for the genus. *Anomala* means anomalous, and refers to the fact that this tree bears single leaves, while the genus is characterized by multiple leaves. *Lowellii* honors Percival Lowell; *cuspidata* refers to the sharp-pointed leaf apex; *greggii* honors botanist Josiah Gregg; and *velutina* refers to the velvety quality of the leaves of this species.

Singleleaf ash is said to occur in extreme northwestern New Mexico, but if so, it is very limited. It also occurs in northeastern Arizona and west to the Grand Canyon, north into Utah and western Colorado, where it becomes treelike in stature. It is readily identified when the characteristic ashlike winged seeds can be found. The leaves are nearly round or somewhat flattened across the bottom. The wood is hard and heavy, coarse-grained, straw colored to light brown. This species appears to cross readily with velvet ash in southwest Utah, where trees with various leaf forms occur.

Lowell ash is known only from central Arizona where it occurs in the oak woodland and upper desert. It grows as a shrub or may become treelike. It may be distinguished from velvet ash by the 4-angled stems that are sometimes winged, by the somewhat broader leaflets, and by the fruits, which are about twice as large as those of velvet ash. It has no importance except as an element in the cover.

Fragrant ash qualifies as a small tree, but it is most often shrublike in our region, where it occurs sparsely in dry situations in the western mountains of New Mexico and around the Grand Canyon in Arizona. It is said to be common in the lower elevations of the Zuni Mountains of New Mexico. It is unusual among ash species in that the flowers have petals and a fragrant odor. Otherwise, the tree will readily be recognized as an ash by the typical fruits, or keys, and the compound leaves with five to seven small leaflets. The

Singleleaf ash

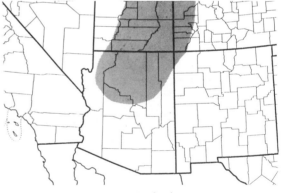

Singleleaf ash

Singleleaf ash

leaves are readily taken by grazing animals and would be of some wildlife value except for the scarcity of the plants. The wood is dense, fine-grained, medium hard, and heavy. The sapwood is light straw colored and the heartwood is medium brown. It has no economic importance.

Gregg ash is listed as occurring in western Texas, Mexico, and in Arizona only in Sycamore Canyon near Ruby in Santa Cruz County. It is sometimes called littleleaf ash, as the leaves are only about 1½ inches long with leaflets from ½ to 3/4 or occasionally 1½ inches long. The wing attached to the seed is broad and much longer than the seed. The hard and heavy wood is brown in color.

Velvet ash occurs in southwest New Mexico from the White Mountains, south and west, in southeastern, central and northwestern Arizona, including the Grand Canyon and north into Utah. The tree grows in association with Arizona walnut in the bottoms of the canyons. It may grow to 40 feet high and a foot or more in diameter. The leaves are compound, with 5 to 9 leaflets to a leaf, similar to white and green ash. The flowers appear before the leaves in the spring, and the large clusters of winged seeds, called keys, develop later in the summer and serve as a good identifying characteristic. The wood is similar to the commercial ash, but is not quite so coarse and hard to work. It is a pinkish straw color, but the supply is too limited to be of any commercial value. The trees are planted as ornamentals in many Southwest and California towns and as far away as South Africa. This plant is well adapted for use in irrigated windbreak plantings in our region.

Velvet ash

Velvet ash

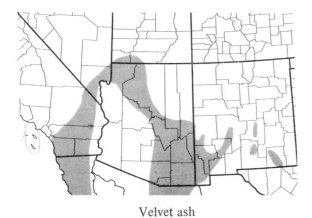

Velvet ash

Fragrant ash

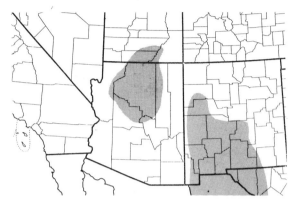

Fragrant ash

Fragrant ash(leaf detail)

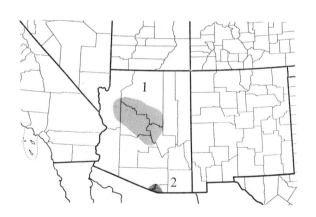

1. Lowell ash
2. Gregg ash

7

BARBERRY FAMILY
(Berberidaceae)

Algerita—*Mahonia trifoliolata*
"Palo amarillo"
Red mahonia—*M. haematocarpa*
Creeping mahonia—*M. repens*
Fremont mahonia—*M. fremontii*
Wilcox mahonia—*M. wilcoxi*
Fendler mahonia—*M. fendleri*
Kofa mahonia—*M. harrisoniana*

The literature concerning this genus is very confused. Some writers consider the name *Berberis* to be proper and others use *Odostemon*. I have chosen to use Mahonia, following Vines. The common names are equally confusing. Creeping mahonia is commonly called oregongrape, a name more properly applied to *Mahonia aquifolia*, State flower of Oregon. Other writers use holly grape as the common name for many of the species, and barberry for some. The genus name honors Bernard W. Mahon, an American horticulturist. *Trifoliolata* refers to 3-parted leaves, *haematocarpa* to the blood-red berries, *repens* to the creeping habit that gives it the common name, and the other species names honor various men.

Algerita is very common in the pinon country of the middle and southern parts of New Mexico and extends into the southeastern corner of Arizona, south into Mexico and east through much of Texas. A large shrub, it is commonly up to 8 feet tall but may reach 10 feet. It is very sturdy and stiff. The leaves are alternate, evergreen, holly-like, 3-parted, and spiny. The small yellow flowers are borne in small clusters on short pedestals at the axils of the leaves. In the fall, the bush is heavily loaded with red berries which make excellent jellies. The seeds are avidly sought by birds, and the stout bushes make good cover for birds and small mammals. Deer are known to eat algerita. The sapwood is quite thick in the larger stems where it is hard, heavy, and a beautiful deep yellow color. A dye can be made from the wood and roots, and the yellow wood makes attractive ornaments. The heartwood is reddish brown and often rotten in larger stems, which are up to 6 inches in diameter.

Red mahonia is quite similar in many respects, except that there may be from 3 to 7 leaflets on a stem, the berries are a darker red color and the growth habit of the shrub appears more open with more slender branches than

Algerita

Algerita

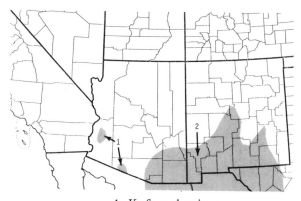

1. Kofa mahonia
2. Algerita

found generally in algerita. The range is broader than that given for algerita. I found a good specimen in Guadalupe Canyon in southwestern New Mexico.

Creeping mahonia is hardly a shrub but is included for sake of completeness and because of abundance in its range. This mahonia occurs in the higher mountains throughout the west, the Guadalupe Mountains of west Texas, and from about 7,000 feet to 10,000 feet in the mountains of our area. It is a low, creeping shrub, seldom over 12 inches high. The alternate 3- to 7-lobed leaves are shaped like holly leaves with weak spines or prickles around the edge. The flowers are yellow, the fruit is black and lustrous, and the stems are only about ½ inch in diameter. It makes good ground cover to protect the soil of the high mountains.

Fremont mahonia is very similar to red mahonia but occurs in a more restricted range. It has inflated dry, dark blueberries in contrast to the red, juicy berries of the red mahonia. The leaflets appear short and broad in contrast to the long, slender leaflets of the latter.

Wilcox mahonia occurs in southeastern Arizona and may appear in similar types in southwestern New Mexico and south into Mexico. It grows in association with Arizona cypress and Arizona madrone in the Chiricahua Mountains. Here it forms a low shrub up to 2 feet high. The compound leaves have 5 to 7 leaflets, generally. They are holly-like in shape and with spines on the margins. The rather large bluish-black fruits are said to be very good to eat.

Kofa Mountain barberry is confined to the Kofa Mountains of southwestern Arizona. It is a small shrub, up to 3 feet tall, with 3 leaflets and bluish-black fruits.

Fendler mahonia is a more northern species. It is said to occur in the mountains of northern New Mexico and Colorado at elevations of up to 8,500 feet. The spiny shrub grows erect and up to about 6 feet tall. The deciduous leaves occur in threes, attached very close to the stem, at which point occur 3 sharp spines. The fruits are very small and red in color.

Red mahonia

Red mahonia

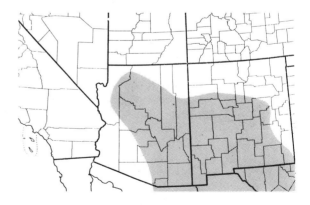

Red mahonia

9

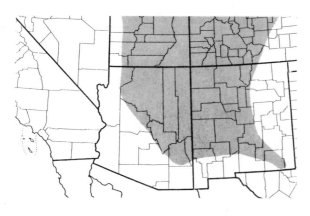

Creeping mahonia

Creeping mahonia

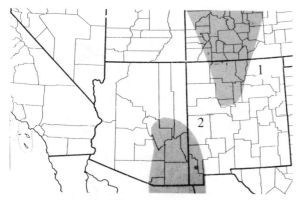

1. Wilcox mahonia
2. Fendler mahonia

Creeping mahonia

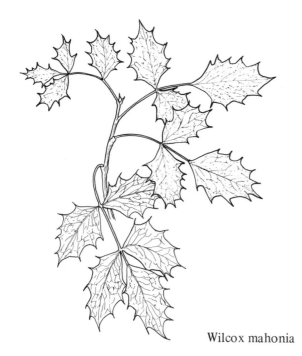

Wilcox mahonia

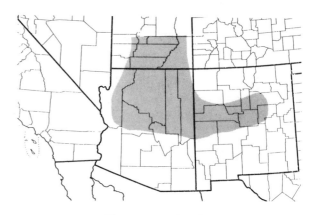

Fremont mahonia

BEECH FAMILY
(Fagaceae)

Arizona white oak—*Quercus arizonica*
"Encino blanco"
Chinquapin oak—*Q. muehlenbergii*
Emory oak—*Q. emoryi*
"Bellota"
Gambel oak—*Q. gambelii*
Gray oak—*Q. grisea*
Mexican blue oak—*Q. oblongifolia*
"Bellota"
Mohr oak—*Q. mohriana*
Netleaf oak—*Q. reticulata*
"Ahoaquahutil"
Palmer canyon live oak—*Q. chrysolepis* var.
    palmeri
Sandpaper oak—*Q. pungens*
Shinnery or shin oak—*Q. havardii*
Shrub live oak—*Q. turbinella*
Silverleaf oak—*Q. hypoleucoides*
"Encino blancho"
Toumey oak—*Q. toumeyi*
Wavyleaf oak—*Q. undulata*

Quercus means beautiful tree in Latin. The meanings of the specific names are as follows: *arizonica* from the State; *muehlenbergii* honors G. H. E. Muehlenberg, botanist; *emoryi* honors Lt. Col. William H. Emory, Southwest explorer; *gambelii* honors Dr. Gambel, early medical doctor; *grisea* means gray, referring to the bark; *oblongifolia* refers to the oblong leaf; *mohriana* honors Charles Mohr, early botanist; *reticulata* refers to the netted leaves; *chrysolepis,* means golden scale—*palmeri* honors Edward Palmer, early plant collector; *pungens* refers to the sharp-pointed leaves; *havardii* honors Valery Havard, botanist; *turbinella* is from turbinate, meaning shaped like a top, and ella, the diminutive form; *hypoleucoides* refers to the whitish or silver color on the under-side of the leaves; *toumeyi* honors James W. Toumey, botanist and forester; *undulata* refers to the wavy margin of the leaves.

Botanists differ on the number of species occurring in that part of the Southwest considered here, but fifteen are listed in this book. Omitted are *Q. ajoensis* from Mesa Verde National Park and the Ajo mountains of Arizona, and *Q. rugosa* from Saguaro National Monument, because none of my references recognized them as valid species. Also omitted are the hybrids.

The oaks under consideration are distributed in our area from the Lower Sonoran Life Zone to the Transition Zone. From the standpoint of food for wildlife, this is the most important genus of all the broadleafed group. For this reason, it is important to list and discuss all species, but to do so in detail would be repetitious and space-consuming. Thus the important material is condensed in the table. This makes the material on each species available for ready comparison.

In the oaks, we have a fortunate combination, for wildlife, of a highly edible and nutritious fruit and edible leaves. This, combined with broad occurrence in the region, makes them very valuable to wildlife. They fulfill the ever-present need for both food and cover. The leaves of many species are browsed heavily by deer, desert bighorn sheep, and elk. The acorns are taken avidly by deer, squirrels, turkeys, javelina, quail, bears, raccoon, band-tailed pigeons, prairie chickens, and even by rodents, coyotes, and foxes.

Oaks in general tend to hybridize where the ranges of species overlap. This leads to variations in leaf form and other botanical characteristics which make positive identification of individual trees difficult. This does not affect their value to wildlife, but it disturbs the botanist. One learns to identify the trees by growth characteristics, habitat, and location in the area, rather than by the leaf shape or acorn shape. All too often, the same tree will carry leaves of widely varying shape. Often a new sprout will have leaves that are much more dentate around the margin than leaves on older growth. Thus, consideration must be given to the general leaf form rather than to a specific leaf.

The largest measured Gambel oak grows in the Gila National Forest in New Mexico. It is 18'3" in circumference, 47' tall, and has a crown spread of 85 feet. Other very large oaks of several species may be found in the canyon bottoms of the Animas and Peloncillo Mountains of New Mexico and the Chiricahua Mountains of Arizona.

Some peculiarities of our oaks might be of interest. Gambel oak is the only oak in our area with the deeply lobed leaves normally associated with oaks. Toumey oak has the smallest leaves of any of our oaks. Shinnery probably has the largest acorns, yet is the smallest plant. Silverleaf oak is least apt to be recognized as an oak because of the long, slender leaves, silvery on the underside. With three exceptions—shinnery, mohr, and chinquapin—the same oaks are found in Arizona as are found in New Mexico. With the many other species to be found in Texas and California it is odd that there is not more difference in the oak flora of the two States.

Arizona white oak

BEECH FAMILY
(Fagaceae)

The following give common names (1), distribution (2), characteristics (3), and uses (4) of the oaks of the Southwest.

ARIZONA WHITE OAK ("Encino blanco").
(2) Arizona in southwest and central parts; N.M. mountains across southern half. Largest oaks are in moist canyons, others grow in oak woodland. (3) Evergreen leaves 1-3" long often wavy-lobed or pointed tipped. Acorn up to 1" long, shallow cup. Stout branches extend at right angles to trunk.
(4) Light pinkish sapwood; very dark red heart. Used for fuel and posts.

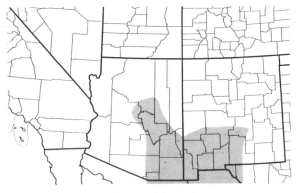

Arizona white oak

Arizona white oak

CHINQUAPIN OAK. (2) Confined to the Guadalupe, Sacramento, Capitan Mts. and one spot near Mora, N.M. Absent from rest of our area. (3) Deciduous leaves, lance-shaped to 6" long, edges wavy, coarse teeth. Small acorn half-enclosed in cup.
(4) Hard and heavy, coarse-grained, light tan in color.

1. Netleaf oak
2. Chinquapin oak

Chinquapin oak

12

Chinquapin oak

Chinquapin oak

EMORY OAK ("Encino"). (2) Mountains of south-west N.M. from Black Range south and west, and in Arizona in southeast and central parts. (3) Leaves persistent through winter, medium-sized, slender with elongated tip but few side points. Small acorn, sweetish, edible, third or more enclosed in cup. Small tree. (4) Light-colored sapwood, gray-brown heart, hard and heavy. Posts and fuel.

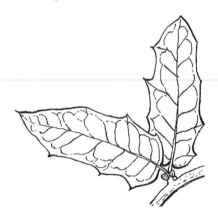

Emory oak

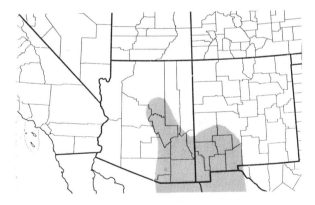

Emory oak

Emory oak

GAMBEL OAK. (2) Widespread throughout the ponderosa pine forests of our area. (3)Deciduous, deeply lobed leaves. Broad, round acorn to 3/4" dia., deep cup. Trees tend to grow in large clumps as large shrubs or singly as trees. (4) Thin white sap, light brown heart, dense and heavy, checks badly in curing. Posts and fuel.

Gambel oak

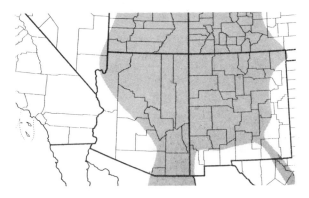

Gambel oak

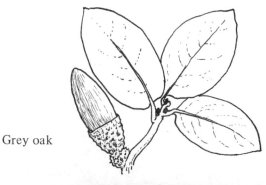

Gambel oak clump

GREY OAK ("Encino prieta"). (2) Uncommon in mts. of southwest and central Arizona, common in piñon-juniper woodland in southern half of N.M. Replaced by Mexican blue oak in extreme southwest. (3) Evergreen leaves, small, oval, smooth margins, gray colored. Small acorn ½" long. Typically a small, round-crowned tree or shrub on dry hillsides. (4) Light straw sap, dark brown heart, hard and heavy, cross-grained. Too small for posts.

Grey oak

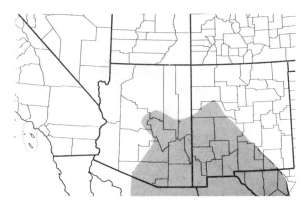

Grey oak

Grey oak

Grey oak--leaf detail

MEXICAN BLUE OAK ("Bellota"). (2) Extreme southwest N.M. on dry hillsides and more common in foothills and mts. of SE Arizona. Also Carlsbad Caverns Nat'l. Park. (3) Leaves evergreen, small, oblong, rounded tip, gray color. Small acorn 1/3 enclosed in cup. Small tree on dry hillsides. Leaves more oblong than in gray oak. (4) Wood gray with prominent silvery rays, hard, heavy, and cross-grained.

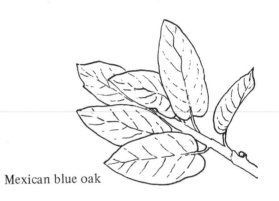

Mexican blue oak

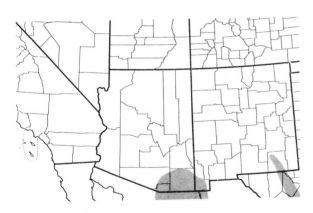

Mexican blue oak

Mexican blue oak

Mexican blue oak--leaf detail

MOHR OAK. (2) Found only in the Guadalupe Mts. of N.M. in our area. (3) Thicket-forming shrub to small tree. Leaves usually small, persistent, oblong, margin nearly entire. Very small acorns up to 2/3 enclosed in cup. (4) Wood too small to use.

Mohr oak

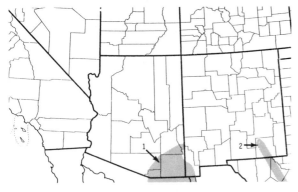

1. Toumey oak
2. Mohr oak

NETLEAF OAK ("Ahoaquahuitl"). (2) Scarce in mts. of southwestern N.M. but more common in SE Ariz. to Coconino Cty. Also SW Texas and Mexico. In mts. and canyons. (3) Leaves evergreen, large broadly rounded, network of raised veins underside. Acorns ½" long, 2 or 3 together on long stalk, cup shallow. Tree med. size, rounded crown. (4) Sapwood white, heart light brown, hard and heavy.

(see map on p. 12)

PALMER CANYON LIVE OAK. (2) Scarce in far southwestern N.M. More common across Arizona to SW Utah and west to southern Calif. (3) Evergreen leaves to 1½" long by ½" wide, entire to nearly round or oblong with many sharp tips on margin. Acorn large to 1½" in large cup taking 2 yrs. to mature. (4) Broad sap white, heart brown, hard and heavy.

Netleaf oak

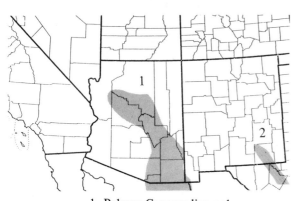

1. Palmer Canyon live oak
2. Sandpaper oak

Palmer Canyon live oak

SANDPAPER OAK. (2) Scarce in southeast N.M. and southern Ariz. in the mts. (3) Evergreen leaves, simple, stiff blades up to 1½" by 3/4" resembling small holly leaves. Small acorn set shallowly in cup. Generally only a shrub. (4) Sapwood white, heart light brown, hard and heavy.

(see map on previous page)

Sandpaper oak

Sandpaper oak

SHINNERY OR SHIN OAK. (2) East of the Pecos River in N.M. and eastward in Texas and Oklahoma on the plains. (3) Low-growing shrub in our area. Deciduous leaves coarsely toothed or lobed. Very large acorn set 1/3 to ½ in cup. (4) Wood too small to use in our area, but may become large enough for posts farther east.

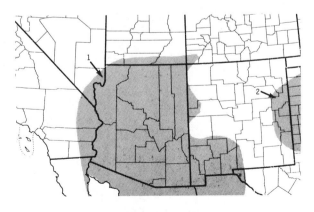

1. Shrub live oak
2. Shinnery oak

Shinnery oak

SHRUB LIVE OAK. (2) Mts. of southwest N.M. from Organs southwestward. Widespread over Ariz. to SW Colo. and southern Utah. (3) Evergreen leaves small and holly-shaped, ½ to 1½" long, narrow and pointed, 1/3 in cup. Generally only a shrub. (4) Tan or yellowish sap, deep brown heart, too small for posts generally.

(see map on previous page)

Shrub live oak

Shrub live oak

SILVERLEAF OAK ("Encino blanco"). (2) Mts. of southwest N.M. from Black Range westward. Mts. of SE Ariz. (3) Persistent leaves, long slender, smooth-margined, silvery underneath, dark green top. Small acorn 1/3 enclosed in cup. Generally a shrub clump. (4) Sap nearly white, heart blackish brown. Too small to use.

Silverleaf oak

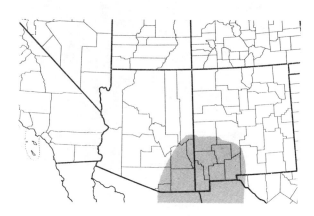

Silverleaf oak

Silverleaf oak

Silverleaf oak--leaf detail

TOUMEY OAK. (2) Very locally in extreme south-west N.M. and southeastern Ariz. (3) Smallest leaves of our oaks, evergreen, oblong, slender, entire margin. Small acorn with shallow cup. Small tree or shrub. (4) Yellowish white to very light tan, brown around knots. Too small to use.

(see map on p. 16)

Wavyleaf oak

WAVYLEAF OAK. (2) Common in pinon-juniper woodland in all our areas. (3) Usually evergreen leaves to 2½" long with wavy margins often curled. Medium acorn set ½ in cup. Occurs as dense brush thickets or occasionally becomes tree. (4) White sap, deep brown heart. Seldom large enough for posts.

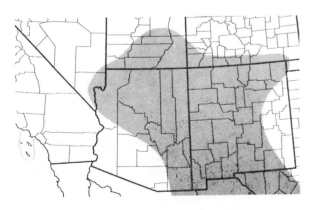

Wavyleaf oak

Wavyleaf oak

19

BIRCH FAMILY
(Betulaceae)

Water birch—*Betula occidentalis*

Betula is a Gaulish word for the birch tree; *occidentalis* means western and is the specific name used by Little. Another name is *B. fontinalis*, which refers to a spring of water. This surely alludes to the tree's favored habitat near the water.

Water birch is closely associated with alder and willows along the streams of northern New Mexico, northeastern Arizona, and on north to Canada. It generally grows in a dense clump of stems up to 25 feet tall, with each stem only a few inches in diameter. The cylindrical conelike fruiting bodies, 1 to 1½ inches long, distinguish birch from alder, with its more nearly ball-like cones. The wood is hard and heavy. The sapwood is white and the heartwood is light brown. It does not occur in large enough pieces to be of any commercial value. The trees furnish shade along the mountain streams and furnish some nesting sites for songbirds.

Water birch

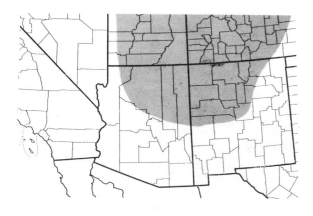

Water birch

Water birch

BIRCH FAMILY
(Betulaceae)

Thinleaf alder—*Alnus tenuifolia*
Arizona or New Mexico alder—*A. oblongifolia*

Thinleaf alder

Alnus is the Latin word for alder, *tenuifolia* means slender-leafed, and *oblongifolia* means oblong-leafed.

Thinleaf alder occurs along the streams in the middle elevations of the mountains throughout northern New Mexico but in Arizona is uncommon in a few mountain ranges. From New Mexico it extends north as far as Canada, in association with willows, water birch, and other typical streamside species. In size it varies from that of a large shrub to a many-stemmed small tree and occurs generally in clumps. The rounded leaves have serrated edges. The flowers are borne in catkins, and the seeds are in small rounded cones, distinct from the long, cylindrical cone-like structures of birch. The bark is thin and reddish brown, and the wood is nearly white when freshly cut, immediately staining to pinkish red on exposure. The pink stain appears to spread from the fresh-cut bark. The wood has no commercial value. The tree furnishes food and dam material for beaver and some cover for other wildlife. It is known to be browsed somewhat by deer and livestock. The largest measured thinleaf alder is 3 feet 5 inches in circumference, 59 feet tall, with a crown spread of 29 feet. It grows in Bandelier National Monument in New Mexico.

Arizona alder, also called New Mexico alder, occurs in New Mexico and in the southeast and central parts of Arizona to Oak Creek. In New Mexico the far northern extension is on the slopes of Mount Taylor, northeast of Grants. It occupies the same niche in the southern mountains of our area as does thinleaf alder in the north.

The botanical features are about the same as thinleaf alder, except that it develops into a medium-sized to large tree up to 80 feet tall and 1 foot to 2 feet in diameter. The wood stains red upon being cut, but not so brightly red as thinleaf alder. The stands of trees are not extensive enough to warrant commercial exploitation. Its wildlife values are the same as for thinleaf alder.

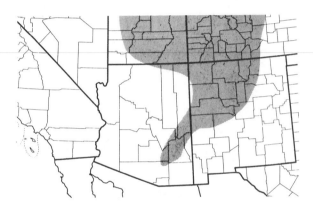
Thinleaf alder

Thinleaf alder in winter

21

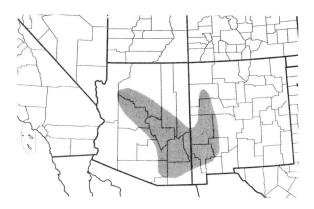

Arizona or New Mexico alder

Arizona or New Mexico alder in winter

BIRCH FAMILY
(*Betulaceae*)

Knowlton hophornbeam—*Ostrya knowltoni*

    Ostrya is from Greek and refers to a tree with hard wood. The species name honors Frank H. Knowlton, an American botanist.
    Knowlton hophornbeam is quite rare and occurs in such widely diverse localities as the Guadalupe and Sacramento Mountains of southeast New Mexico, along both rims of the Grand Canyon, and locally in southeastern Utah and southwestern Texas. It grows in the moist canyons of the oak woodland, pinon-juniper and lower ponderosa pine zones, where it is usually a shrub or small tree. The leaves are alternate, simple, finely serrate along the edges, deciduous, and up to 2½ inches long. The inconspicuous flowers occur at or just before the time of leaf growth in the spring, in small clusters at the tips of the branches. The beechlike fruiting bodies are like small conelets, up to 1½ inches long with baglike papery bracts, in each of which is a small nutlet. The gray bark peels off in long strips. The wood is very hard, tough, and durable, and light reddish brown in color. It is not abundant enough to be of commercial value.

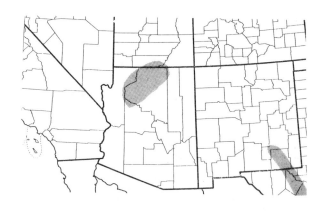

Knowlton hophornbeam

BOX FAMILY
(Buxaceae)

"Jojoba" or goat nut—*Simmondsia chinensis*

The generic name honors Thomas Williams Simmonds, botanist. The specific name is sometimes given as *californica.* In the field jojoba might be confused with Wright silktassel except for the altitudinal distribution. Jojoba grows in the foothills in the 1,500- to 5,000-foot range, and Wright silktassel is a shrub of the pinon-juniper zone above 5,000 feet. Both are shrubs with thick leathery leaves, but the leaves of jojoba have very short stems or none. The leaves are 1 to 1½ inches long and ½ to 3/4 inch wide, opposite, pointed, and evergreen. The male flowers are borne in clusters in the axils of the leaves. The female flowers occur singly, about ½ to 3/4 inch across, and are stalked. The seed pod splits open from the pointed top, and the single seed is acornlike and short-pointed. The shrub is a low, rounded plant, sometimes as much as 7 feet high. It is a valuable browse plant taken by domestic stock and deer. The nuts are edible and have been an important source of food for Indians in the past. The stems are too small to produce usable wood, but the wood is dense, hard, and light brown in color.

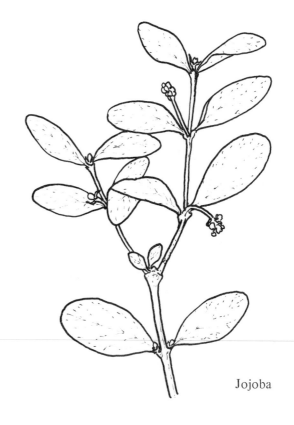

Jojoba

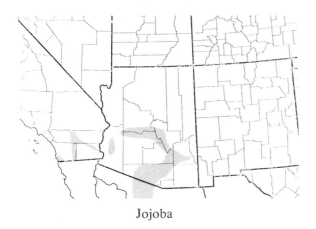

Jojoba

Jojoba

23

BUCKTHORN FAMILY
(Rhamnaceae)

Lotewood condalia—*Condalia obtusifolia*
"Abrojo"
Southwestern condalia or greythorn—
    Condalia lycioides
"Crucillo"
Bitter condalia—*Condalia globosa*
"Tecomblate"
Knifeleaf condalia—*Condalia spathulata*
Mexican bluewood condalia—*Condalia mexicana*
"Bindo"
Warnock condalia—*C. warnockii* var.
    kearneyana

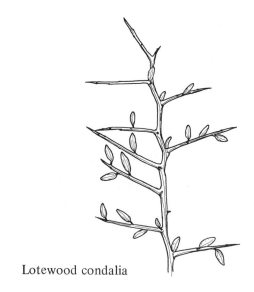

Lotewood condalia

The naming of the condalias is confusing and, as is mentioned by Vines, should probably be revised to reduce *C. lycioides* to a variety or synonym of *C. obtusifolia* and to reduce *C. mexicana* to a variety of *C. spathulata*. I have followed Vines in his classification. *Condalia* honors Antonio Condal, a Spanish physician. *Obtusifolia* refers to the obtuse apex of the leaf; *lycioides* refers to the lycium-like foliage; *globosa* is the Latin form of globose; *spathulata* refers to the spatulate leaves.

Vines points out that in following condalia from east to west, the eastern plants are most like *C. obtusifolia* and the farther west one goes the more the plants become like *C. lycioides*. From my observation, I feel that the eastern form is more leafy and the western form is more starkly gray, but this could be a seasonal change. The form seen on the Pecos drainage north of Roswell was a low, leafy, dark-colored bush, while the form seen from Tucson westward was a tall open-growing shrub, very spiny, light gray in color, and almost leafless. The flowers are very small, whitish green, and the dark blue or black berries are scarcely ¼ inch in diameter. The leaves are up to 3/4 inch long and narrow. The bushes make very good nesting sites for desert birds and very often contain a nest. The thorny nature of the bush makes it very hard for a predator to catch or molest the nesting bird.

Bitter condalia fits much the same description as the above, except that the small, black berries are very bitter if chewed.

Knifeleaf condalia can be readily distinguished by its very small leaves, less than ½ inch long and very narrow. The shrub becomes as much as 10 feet tall, rounded in form, and impenetrable. The small purple

Lotewood condalia with bird nest

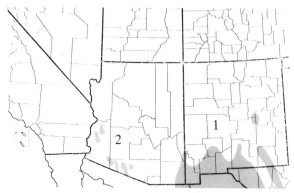

1. Lotewood condalia
2. Bitter condalia

24

fruits are juicy and edible. The bush presents a dark green appearance rather than the gray appearance of the graythorn or southwestern condalia.

Mexican bluewood condalia has larger leaves than knifeleaf condalia, with rigid branches and right-angled branchlets ending in spines. The short-beaked fruit is black.

Lotewood and southwestern condalia range from Texas west across the southern third of New Mexico, across southern Arizona into southern California and south into Mexico. Bitter condalia is found in southwestern Arizona and northwestern Mexico. Knifeleaf condalia occurs in western Texas, southern New Mexico and southern California, and Mexican condalia ranges across southern New Mexico and southeastern Arizona, south into Mexico. Warnock condalia is listed as occurring in Saguaro National Monument.

The wood of the condalia is extremely hard, heavy, and dense. The sapwood is thin and straw-colored, while the heartwood is very deep brown, cross-grained and brittle.

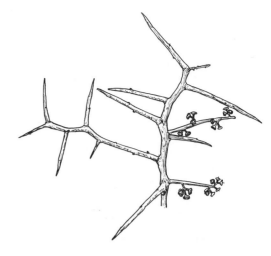

Southwestern condalia in winter

Southwestern condalia

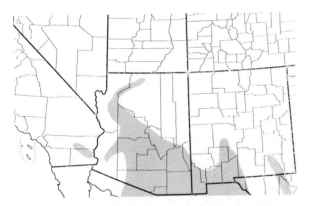

Southwestern condalia

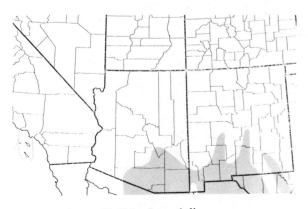

Knifeleaf condalia

Knifeleaf condalia

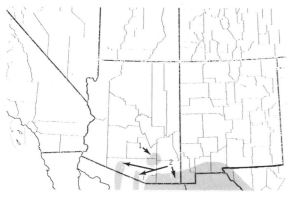

1. Warnock condalia
2. Mexican bluewood condalia

Knifeleaf condalia

Deerbrush

BUCKTHORN FAMILY
(Rhamnaceae)

Fendler ceanothus—*Ceanothus fendleri*
Desert ceanothus—*C. greggii*
Deerbrush—*C. integerrimus*
Martin ceanothus—*C. martini*
Snowbrush—*C. velutinus*

Ceanothus is the ancient Greek.
Fendleri honors August Fendler, a German
botanist who explored New Mexico;
greggi honors botanist Gregg; *integerrimus*
refers to the entire, unbroken margins of the
leaves; *martini* honors a man; and *velutinus*
means velvety.

Fendler ceanothus ranges through the
mountains of our area in the upper edge of
the pinon-juniper zone through the ponderosa pine zone. It is particularly abundant
in Lincoln National Forest of north-central
New Mexico and on the Coconino and
Prescott Forests of west-central Arizona. It
is a shrub 3 or more feet high in our area
and sometimes appears abundantly following
fire, as in the case of a burn on the west
side of Capitan Mountain in New Mexico.
The small, whitish flowers occur in clusters
at the ends of the branches. The reddish-
brown fruits are somewhat 3-lobed. The
foliage is sparse and the stems are often
spine-pointed at the tips. The leaves are
alternate. The shrub is very heavily utilized
by deer in our area and is valuable for
domestic stock.

Desert ceanothus occurs in southern
New Mexico and from southeastern Arizona
through the center to the Kaibab plateau.
The botanical characteristics are very similar
to Fendler ceanothus except that the

Deerbrush

26

branches are more silvery white and much stiffer, with stiff sharp spines. The leaves are opposite. This shrub is utilized so heavily by deer that it is unusual to see a specimen which is not severely hedged. As a result, it is generally seen as a closely cropped, rounded shrub 1 to 2 feet high.

Deerbrush is quite a different shrub. The white flowers are borne in a large, showy terminal cluster on long, thin stems. The alternate leaves are 3-ribbed, broadly ovate or oblong, up to 3 inches long. The shrub is open-growing and attains a height up to 10 feet or more. Handsome examples can be seen at the lower edge of the ponderosa pine zone in the Chiricahua Mountains of southeastern Arizona. It occurs in the Pacific Coast States, through Nevada and through the mountains of Arizona, but is scarce in New Mexico.

Martin ceanothus is reported to occur in Utah, northern Arizona, and Nevada. The branches are unarmed and the leaves are larger than those of Fendler ceanothus, rounded and toothed. Lack of spiny tips on the branches subject the shrub to over-grazing.

Snowbrush is quite similar to deerbrush but the shrub is smaller. It extends into Colorado from the north so is not common in our area.

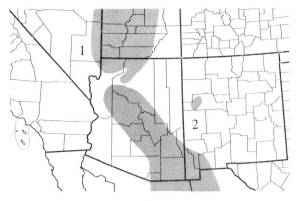

1. Martin ceanothus
2. Deerbrush

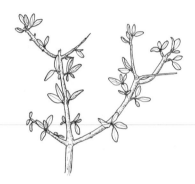

Desert ceanothus

Desert ceanothus

Fendler ceanothus

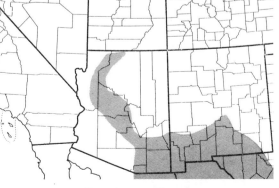

Desert ceanothus

BUCKTHORN FAMILY
(*Rhamnaceae*)

Javelina-brush–*Microrhamnus ericoides*
"Tecomblate"

    Microrhamnus refers to a plant similar to buckthorn but small, and *ericoides* refers to the small leaves like those of *Erica*.
    Javelina-brush occurs sparsely across southern New Mexico from the Guadalupe Mountains in the east to the extreme southwestern corner, and in southeastern Arizona. I found it on the east side of the Peloncillo Mountains. Here it was a small shrub about 2 feet high, growing in a small clump on a dry, gravelly hillside. It was conspicuous because of the black appearance of the bush. The stems are very black and the leaves are so small that they blend with the stems. The shrub is spiny. The sapwood is creamy white and the heartwood is deep lavender, hard, heavy, and dense. The shrub has no wildlife significance except that it makes fine escape cover for quail and small mammals.

Javelina-brush

Javelina-brush

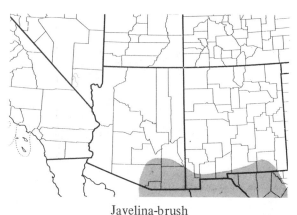

Javelina-brush

BUCKTHORN FAMILY
(*Rhamnaceae*)

Birchleaf buckthorn–*Rhamnus betulaefolia*
California buckthorn–*R. californica*
Hollyleaf buckthorn–*Rhamnus crocea*
Smith buckthorn–*Rhamnus smithi*

    Rhamnus is an ancient name for buckthorn. *Betulaefolia* means birchleaf; *crocea* means yellow or saffron; and *smithi* was named for B. H. Smith, who first found it

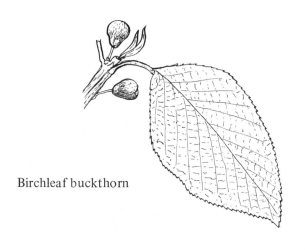

Birchleaf buckthorn

at Pagosa Springs, Colorado.

Birchleaf buckthorn occurs in the mountains of the southwestern part of New Mexico, and in southeastern Arizona. The variety *obovata* extends northwest through central Arizona to the Grand Canyon. It occurs as a large, rounded shrub with many straight, slender stems up to about 2 inches in diameter, or has been reported to make a small tree. The deciduous leaves are oblong, or obovate in the variety. The leaves are up to 4 inches long with finely toothed edges not rolled under. The berries are small and 3-seeded. It is not sufficiently abundant to be of wildlife value in our area.

California buckthorn is an evergreen shrub generally about 6 feet tall, which may become treelike. It is said to occur in southwestern New Mexico and across into southeastern and central Arizona. It grows in the woodland zones and up into the ponderosa pine zone. The leaves are oval, up to 3 inches long, leathery, with the edges slightly rolled under. Small greenish flowers occur in a small cluster at the base of the leaf stem, and the berries are black when ripe, with 3 seeds.

Hollyleaf buckthorn does not occur in New Mexico but in Arizona, southern California and south into Lower California. It is found in the chaparral zone and lower part of the ponderosa pine zone. I found it associated with shrub live oak in the mountains south of Prescott. It is generally a medium-sized shrub to about 8 feet tall but is said to become treelike. The bark at the base of old trunks is dark and broken in a ridged pattern, but on the long, slender, young branches it is smooth and gray. The sapwood is light yellow and the heart is light brown in color. The leaves are nearly round, bright, shiny evergreen, about 1 inch in diameter, with considerable size variation. The berries are red and small.

Smith buckthorn was first found in southern Colorado. It is not known to occur in New Mexico except in the extreme southern part of the State in the Guadalupe Mountains. It is said to be a rounded, densely leafy shrub of variable height up to 15 feet. The leaves are small and the small berries usually have only two nutlets.

None of the buckthorns are considered to be valuable, either for domestic stock or game. They contribute to cover, but in the areas where they typically occur, cover is abundantly supplied by plants of more value to game and to domestic stock.

Birchleaf buckthorn

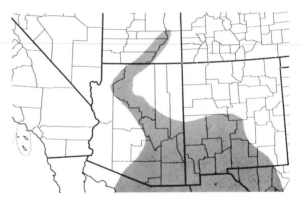

Birchleaf buckthorn

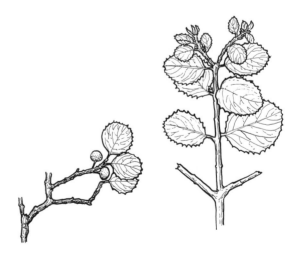

Hollyleaf buckthorn

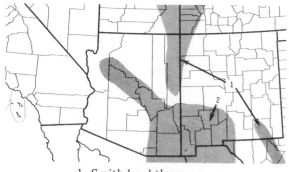

1. Smith buckthorn
2. California buckthorn

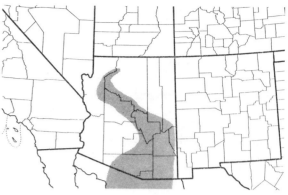

Hollyleaf buckthorn

BURSERA FAMILY
(Burseraceae)

Elephant-tree—*Bursera microphylla*
"Torote" or "Copal"

The genus name honors Joachim Burser, German botanist, and the species name means little leaf.

This is a very rare tree growing in the desert in various places along the Arizona-Mexico and the California-Baja California borders. It grows along sandy washes and cannot withstand cold weather. The trunk is large at the base but tapers rapidly. The limbs follow the same pattern, which gives them the appearance of an elephant trunk, thus the common name. The leaves are compound with up to 20 small leaflets, similar in appearance to a mesquite. The small, red fruits are attached by short stems to the leaf axils. The wood is hard, close-grained, and pale yellow.

Elephant-tree

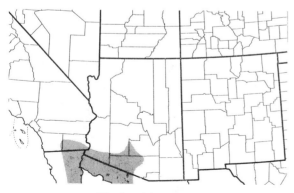

Elephant-tree

Elephant-tree

CACTUS FAMILY
(Cactaceae)

"Saguaro"–*Cereus giganteus* or *Carnegiea giganteus*

Organpipe cactus– *Cereus thurberi* or *Lemair eocereus thurber*

"Organo" or "Tarritos"

Senita–*Cereus schottii* or *Lophocereus schottii*

Authors disagree concerning the genus name for these three treelike cacti. I have chosen to follow Little in this publication. (For anyone wanting more detail, there are several good publications concerning the cacti of the Southwest; see the bibliography.) *Cereus* is the classical Latin name for the genus, and *giganteus* means large, and the application is obvious. The other two specific names honor men.

None of these cacti occur any place in our area except Arizona. Saguaro grows in a large area of central, southern, and western Arizona from Tucson to the Colorado River and west into southeastern California and in Sonora, Mexico. Some of the best stands are in the two sections of Saguaro National Monument near Tucson. These are the largest of the cacti in the United States. They are usually from 20 to 35 feet high but may reach 50 or more feet. They become 1 foot or more in diameter, with a single trunk and 1 to several branches. The trunk has many prominent ridges, each profusely thorny. The flowers occur as a coronet around the top of the trunk or large branches, opening only at night. They are white, large with waxy petals. The fruits are red, fleshy, sweet, and edible, and special candies are made of them.

The wood consists of a skeleton of rods like large dowel pins, extending from the base to the top of the trunk. The wood is soft and light tan in color. Woodpeckers drill many holes in the older trunks, which are taken over as nesting sites by many desert birds and small mammals.

Organpipe cactus may be found in Organ Pipe Cactus National Monument in southern Arizona on the Mexican border. The very rare Senita is found only in the Monument and in Mexico.

Saguaro

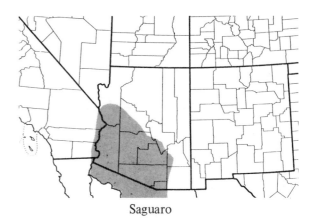

Saguaro

Organpipe cactus

Senita (in foreground)

Organpipe cactus

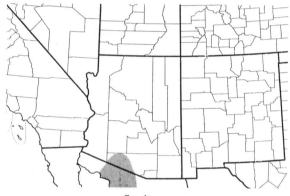

Senita

CACTUS FAMILY
(Cactaceae)

Common cholla—*Opuntia imbricata*
"Xoconostli"
"Tasajo"—*Opuntia spinosior*
Jumping cholla—*Opuntia fulgida*
"Velas de Coyote"
Staghorn cholla—*Opuntia versicolor*
Buckhorn cholla—*Opuntia acanthocarpa*

The cacti of the Southwest have been very adequately covered by Lyman Benson and others, but no book on trees and shrubs of the area would be complete without at least brief mention of the Opuntias. *Opuntia* is from Opus, a town in Greece. *Imbricata* refers to the overlapping edges of the joints, so characteristic of our common cholla or walking stick cactus. *Spinosior* refers to the extremely spiny character of the western variety of cholla. *Fulgida* means shining and refers to the shiny character of the spines. *Versicolor* refers to the various colors of the

Common cholla

flowers. *Acanthocarpa* is derived from *acantho*, thorn or hook; and *carpa*, meaning seed.

The opuntias named above, along with some less common ones, make up much of the shrubby cover of vast areas of the Southwest. Common cholla is widespread over the Sonoran zones of New Mexico and spreads up into the lower edge of the Transition Zone. It occurs northward in Colorado as far as Pueblo. Generally found as a shrub up to about 6 feet high, in favorable locations it makes a small tree with branched trunk up to about 10 inches in diameter. The small dead branches are hollow, with a network of lenticular holes. This gives a cured stick a lacelike appearance. Such sticks are used as canes and in ornamental woodwork. The large old branches and main trunk have hollow cores, but the lenticular holes are nearly or completely filled. The resulting wood is hard, heavy, and dense, light to medium brown in color, and suitable for making ornamental objects.

Tasajo is found in southwestern New Mexico and in the southeastern quarter of Arizona, south into Mexico. The appearance and growth habit is very similar to common cholla, and it appears to occupy about the same niche in its range.

Jumping cholla will be distinguished from other chollas immediately. One sees it around Tucson and north along Highway 80 to Florence, where it is very common. The joints are crowded around the tops of the stems and are so densely thorny that they appear to be covered with cotton threads. The bright straw-colored spines are about 1 inch long and barbed. They are difficult to extract once they become embedded in the flesh. The cylinders even on the old trunks appear to be hollow, so that the only wood produced is that of the lacelike outer framework.

Neither staghorn nor buckhorn cholla occur in New Mexico. Staghorn occurs in southern Arizona, and buckhorn occurs in southern and western Arizona and on into Utah, Nevada, and southern California. Both form large shrubs or small trees up to 15 feet tall. Both are branched but buckhorn seems to branch more like deer antlers. The branches of buckhorn are about 1 inch in diameter while those of staghorn are about ½ to 1 inch thick; thus both are much more slender than the other three chollas described.

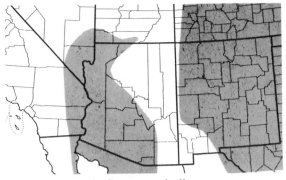

1. Common cholla
2. Buckhorn cholla

"Tasajo"

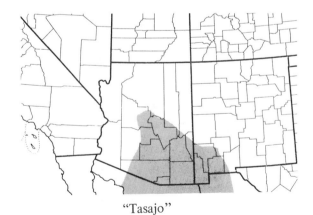

"Tasajo"

Chollas invade pasture land, and if the stand becomes dense, the livestock have trouble in feeding and the rancher finds it hard to herd the cattle. The fruits and seeds are eaten by cattle, antelope, desert bighorn sheep, deer, and many other mammals and birds. The plants make ideal escape cover for quail, songbirds, and small mammals.

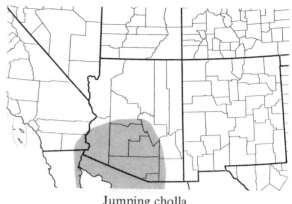

Jumping cholla

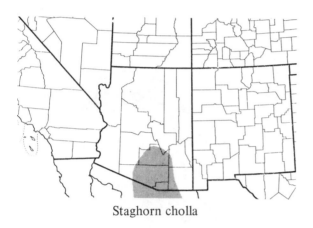

Staghorn cholla

Staghorn cholla

CALTROP FAMILY
(*Zygophyllaceae*)

Creosotebush—*Larrea tridentata*
"Gobernadora." "Guamis"

The generic name honors J.A. de Larrea, a Spanish promoter of science. *Tridentata*, in this case, describes the stamen stalk or may refer to the 3-angled seeds.

This is a widespread shrub, occurring from southern California across southern Nevada and southern Utah to southern Colorado and west Texas and south across Arizona and New Mexico to Mexico. It most frequently occurs on the deep, gravelly soils of outwash fans between the lower edges of the foothills and the bottom of the valley. It is such an efficient user of the water supply that frequently it is difficult to find any other plants growing in association with it. Bur sage accompanies it in some areas. It covers vast areas in its range.

Creosotebush

The small, short-stalked, solitary flowers are yellow, with 5 petals. The fruit is covered densely with fine white hairs. The small leaves are evergreen, bright green, and leathery, occur in pairs united at the base, and are resinous. The crushed leaves give off an odor reminiscent of creosote.

The shrub appears to be worthless as far as use by game or domestic stock is concerned. Scaled quail use it for cover because it is present on so much of their range. The fact that it is present on the range prevents better plants from growing. It does not grow closely enough spaced to serve as a good soil protector. It is difficult to reseed if it is cleared away. The shrub usually grows to about 5 feet tall; the stems are more open and seldom over 1½ inches in diameter. The clumps that I have seen growing in southeastern California, across the Colorado river from Yuma, Arizona, average nearly 10 feet tall but the stems are slender.

Creosotebush

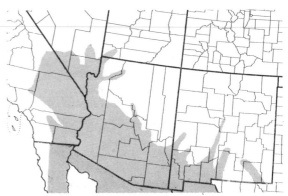

Creosotebush

COMPOSITE FAMILY
(Compositae)

Big sagebrush—*Artemisia tridentata*
Silver sagebrush—*A. cana*
Sand sagebrush—*A. filifolia*
"Estafiate"
Black sagebrush—*A. nova*
Fringed sagebrush—*A. frigida*

Artemisia was the wife of Mausolus, king of Carla, and was named for Artemis, the Greek goddess of the moon and of wild places and wild animals. I don't know why the name was chosen for our sagebrush. *Tridentata* refers to the three dents at the apex of the leaves; *cana* refers to the silvery gray hairs on the leaves; *filifolia* refers to the threadlike leaves; *nova* means new, a newly named species; *frigida* refers to the bleak and frigid regions of Siberia where Willdenow found his type specimen. There are several other species of *Artemisia* in our area, but they tend to be half-shrubs or are rare.

Big sagebrush

A large portion of northwestern New Mexico and northern Arizona lies in the southern extension of the sagebrush or basin desert. Sagebrush occurs over a large part of the western United States in vast areas covering over 100,000,000 acres. In our area, the plant association typically includes big sagebrush, rabbitbrush, black greasewood, winterfat, fourwing saltbush, shadscale, and various species of grass and weeds.

Antelope, mule deer, and elk occur in the sagebrush flats to come extent. Antelope prefer more open rangeland, and deer prefer the adjoining hilly ground where pinon and juniper and associated species furnish more desirable cover. Elk are normally found in higher mountains, but come down in severe winters to feed in sagebrush country. The leaves, twigs and seeds are eaten by deer and Barbary sheep, and antelope graze on leaves and stems.

Sagebrush is readily recognized by the gray-green color of the leaves, the shrubby appearance of the plants, generally about 3 to 5 feet tall, and the rank smell of oil of sage, which is almost overpowering as the leaves are crushed or bruised. The flowers, and later the seeds, occur in long, showy, terminal spikes. The woody stems produce an attractive, light-brown wood, used locally for small ornaments and jewelry, but is never large enough to be of any commercial importance.

Silver sagebrush is sometimes called white sagebrush and is widely distributed in the mountains of our area. It is sometimes found mixed with big sagebrush where moisture conditions are more favorable, and has one of the highest altitudinal ranges of any of the true shrubs of this genus. The shrub grows to a height of 5 feet, has long, slender, silvery leaves and long, terminal spikes of flowers and seeds.

Sand sagebrush is usually found at relatively low elevations and always on sandy sites, exemplified by the stands of the species found in the sandhills of eastern New Mexico and on the sandy plains west of the Rio Grande in central New Mexico. It also occurs in Arizona, Utah and Colorado, and east into Texas. The leaves are almost hairlike, the plant grows to a height of about 4 feet, and the seeds are borne in long, terminal spikes.

Black sagebrush is often associated with big sagebrush but occurs on the shallower soils where it may occur in solid stands but is surrounded by pure stands of big sagebrush on the deeper soils. It is easily mistaken for big sagebrush but is usually much shorter in

Big sagebrush

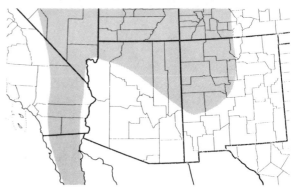

Big sagebrush
Black sagebrush

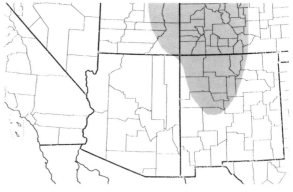

Silver sagebrush

growth form. It is used as an indicator of poor, shallow soils.

Fringed sagebrush is hardly a shrub but does have a woody base. In this it is similar to the several other species of *Artemisia* not described. It is included because of its wide range and importance. It grows on the high plains near the mountains and in the high mountain parks or drier portions of the high mountain valleys. Often considered an indicator of overuse by livestock, it is given a good rating for use by game and is considered an indicator of good antelope range on the high plains. It seldom grows more than about 1 foot tall, is bushy with silvery green leaves, and seeds borne in terminal spikes.

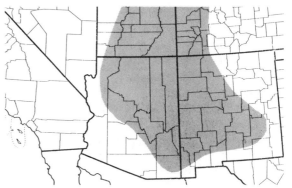

Sand sagebrush

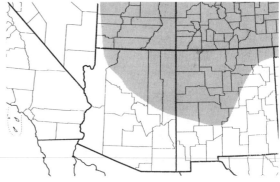

Fringed sagebrush

COMPOSITE FAMILY

(Compositae)

Seepwillow baccharis—*Baccharis glutinosa* "Jarilla, Batemonte, Chilca, Hierba de Pasmo"
Broom baccharis—*Baccharis sarothroides* "Hierba de Pasmo"
Emory baccharis—*Baccharis emoryi*
Arizona baccharis—*Baccharis thesioides*
Yerbadepasmo—*Baccharis pteronioides*

Baccharis is derived from a Greek word. The meanings of the specific names are as follows: *glutinosa* refers to the sticky leaves; *sarothroides* refers to its resemblance to a species of the St. John's-wort family; *emoryi* honors the early Southwest explorer, Emory; *thesioides* is from Greek *thes* meaning divine; *pteronioides* refers to the winged seeds.

Many other species of *Baccharis* occur in the West. Some are better classified as half-shrubs.

Seepwillow baccharis occurs in the Lower Sonoran desert regions of New Mexico and Arizona and along the Colorado River drainage through Arizona to California, northward into Nevada and Utah. It is generally found along stream or ditch banks or along the roads where a little extra moisture drains from the pavement. It grows as a shrub, usually about 6 feet high but may grow to 12 feet on good sites. A large number of virtually unbranched

Seepwillow baccharis

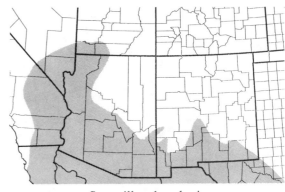

Seepwillow baccharis

37

stems rise from the root, similar to a bamboo plant. The leaves, bright green, sticky, strongly 3-nerved, up to 6 inches long and about ½-inch wide, are pointed and toothed along the edges. The flowers are terminal, yellow, and showy. The fruits have white, showy bristles. The stems are woody but never much more than 1 inch in diameter.

Broom baccharis differs from seepwillow in that the leaves are very minute, giving the stems the appearance of broom straws. The growth form is similar to seepwillow and the shrub occupies much the same niche in Arizona as does seepwillow in New Mexico.

Emory baccharis occurs in much the same area and in the same sites as seepwillow, but it is a more branched shrub with smaller leaves.

Arizona baccharis occurs in a higher elevation range in southern New Mexico and southern Arizona than does seepwillow. The plant seldom exceeds 6 feet in height and is less closely associated with watery sites. The terminal flower and fruiting heads are less conspicuous than are those of seepwillow.

Yerbadepasmo occurs in Texas and Mexico, locally in Arizona, and in the Guadalupe Mountains and Organ Mountains of New Mexico. It is a low-growing shrub of the dry hillsides in the 3,000- to 5,000-foot elevation range. The leaves are very small and clustered along the many-branched stems; the straw-colored flowers are borne at the leaf axils and terminally.

All the species of *Baccharis* are virtually worthless for grazing. Some species furnish a little emergency feed. They serve to bind the soil along stream banks and as cover for wildlife. The woody stems are not large enough to be useful.

Seepwillow baccharis

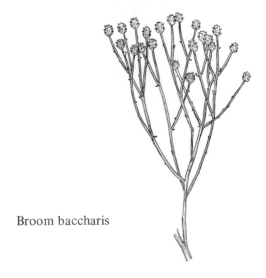

Broom baccharis

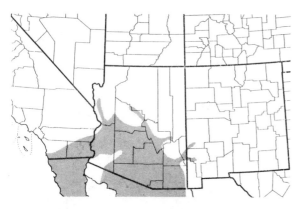

Broom baccharis

Broom baccharis

38

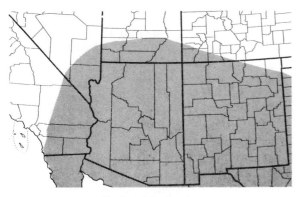

Emory baccharis

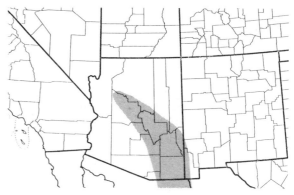

Arizona baccharis

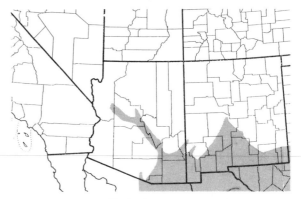

Yerbadepasmo

COMPOSITE FAMILY
(Compositae)

Rubber rabbitbrush or chamisa—*Chryso-*
  thamnus nauseosus
Southwest rabbitbrush—*C. pulchellus*
Douglas rabbitbrush—*C. viscidiflorus*
Greene's rabbitbrush—*C. greenei*
Vasey rabbitbrush—*C. vaseyi*
Dwarf rabbitbrush—*C. depressus*
Rabbitbrush—*C. biglovii*
Desert rabbitbrush—*C. paniculatus*
Flaxleaf rabbitbrush—*C. linifolius*
Rabbitbrush—*C. mohavensis*
Rabbitbrush—*C. stenophyllus*
Rabbitbrush—*C. graveolens*

Chrysothamnus may be divided into
chryso, meaning yellow, and *thamnus*, Greek
for shrub. The species names have meanings
as follows: *nauseosus* refers to the evil smell
of the leaves; *pulchellus* means beautiful;
viscidiflorus refers to the sticky substances on
leaves and flowers; *greenei, vaseyi, biglovii*
are names that honor men; *depressus* means
small or depressed; *paniculatus* refers to
flowering in panicles; *linifolius* refers to the
narrow leaves; *mohavensis*, occurs in the
Mohave Desert; *stenophyllus* refers to long,
slender leaves; *graveolens*, heavy-scented.
Botanists have listed as many as 70
species of rabbitbrush in the West. The ones
listed above are said to occur in one or more

Rubber rabbitbrush or chamisa

of the national parks or monuments of the region or are known to be present in our area. Some are listed as varieties by some authors. Few field workers can distinguish among the species, nor do they find it necessary to do so. All are more or less strong or evil smelling, all have more or less showy yellow flowers in autumn. Most of them grow on seepy, salty, or alkaline soils. Most are indicators of over-grazing and few have significant value for domestic stock, but rubber rabbitbrush is considered valuable for deer, at least in Utah, where it is used in range improvement programs. Rubber rabbitbrush tends to grow well on the newly disturbed soil along highways and it makes, along with purple asters, a beautiful scene in the autumn.

COMPOSITE FAMILY
(Compositae)

American tarbush—*Flourensia cernua*
"Hojasen"

The meaning of *Flourensia* was not found but *cernua* refers to the drooping flower heads.

American tarbush is an indicator of the Chihuahuan Desert and occurs in southern New Mexico, southeastern Arizona, and Texas. The shrub is generally about 3 feet tall but may reach a height of 6 feet. It grows in association with creosotebush in many areas, although the latter often forms pure stands on gravelly outwash fans.

The simple, alternate leaves are persistent, bright, shiny green, but somewhat resinous. They are generally about 1 inch long by ½ inch wide, pointed at the tip and base. The flowers are borne in the upper leaf axils or terminally, are small, yellow, and nodding. The very hairy fruiting bodies are very small and somewhat flattened. The young twigs are light-brown and resinous.

Tarbush has little or no value except as soil cover. Efforts have been made to find ways to control it and encourage its replacement by more valuable forage species. The inhospitable desert climate, however, makes this difficult to achieve.

Rabbitbrush in general is readily distinguished by its slender gray-green leaves, shrubby growth form, rarely over 6 feet in height, and the great profusion of light yellow flowers that crown the bushes in early autumn. The light-brown wood is very similar to that of big sage. Rabbitbrush in one species or another is found from British Columbia to Mexico and west Texas to Baja California. No distribution map is needed.

The Spanish names, "chamisa," "chamiso," or "chamiza," simply mean brush. This becomes confusing, as so many common names do, since the name is applied to at least one brush species in each locality. Often there is little resemblance between the species so honored.

Rubber rabbitbrush appears superficially similar to horsebush. See the description of horsebush for the distinctions.

American tarbush

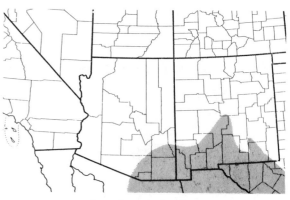

American tarbush

American tarbush

COMPOSITE FAMILY
(Compositae)

Burrobrush-*Hymenoclea monogyra*

 The genus name is from Greek *hymen*, membrane, and *kleio*, to close. In the species name, *mono* means "one" and *gyra* means "whorl of wings."
 Burrobrush occurs in the desert country from the Mojave in western Arizona, across south-central Arizona to the Chihuahuan desert of New Mexico. It grows along arroyos and sandy stream banks, where the shrub may reach a height of about 6 feet. The simple, alternate leaves are about 3 inches long and very slender. The tufted, silvery white flowers occur in the axils of the upper leaves and terminally. The very small fruiting body has up to 12 silvery white wings. The plant is valuable only as ground cover.

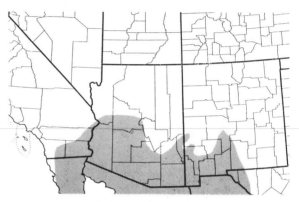
Burrobrush

COMPOSITE FAMILY
(Compositae)

Gray horsebush—*Tetradymia canescens*

 Tetradymia is from a Greek word signifying the four-flowered heads. *Canescens* refers to the gray hairiness.
 Gray horsebush is listed as occurring from New Mexico westward to California and north to Canada. It generally is found on dry, rocky, sunny hillsides or sandy places. It could be classed as a half-shrub, as it is woody below and herbaceous above. It grows to 3 feet in height and has somewhat persistent small, narrow leaves that are covered with silvery hairs. The flowers occur on the ends of the branches in groups of four and are yellow in

Gray horsebush

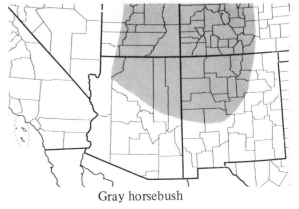
Gray horsebush

41

color. At first the twigs are covered with silvery hairs, but later they have shreddy bark that exposes grayish bark beneath.

Horsebush and rubber rabbitbrush appear to be superficially similar and might be confused where they grow together. However, horsebush appears light gray in winter, the smaller branchlets are crooked and rough because of enlarged nodes, and the seed capsules split into 4 sections, each about 3/8" long. Rabbitbrush has light-greenish branches that are smooth and straight and the seed capsules split into 5 parts, each only about 1/8" long.

Horsebush is listed as being of little or no value for browse but serves as cover for the soil.

Gray horsebush (detail)

COMPOSITE FAMILY
(Compositae)

Parish goldeneye—*Viguiera deltoides* var.
parishii

The genus name honors L. G. A. Viguier, a French botanist. *Deltoides* refers to the shape of the leaves and *parishii* honors W. E. Parish.

Parish goldeneye, or desert sunflower, as it is sometimes called, is another of the desert plants that could be included in the half-shrub group, but is listed as a shrub that grows to a height of about 2½ feet. It occurs in the Mojave Desert of southern Nevada, in western Arizona, and southeast California, where it grows on rocky slopes. The leaves may be opposite on the lower part of the stem and alternate higher. They are small, appear half-folded, are dull green and covered with rough hairs. The very pretty, conspicuous flowers occur on long terminal stems not unlike sunflowers. They are yellow with rays up to 1 inch long. The plant is not known to have any value.

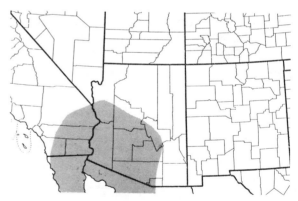

Parish goldeneye

COMPOSITE FAMILY
(Compositae)

Brickellias—*Brickellia* spp.
Bursage—*Franseria* spp.
Snakeweeds—*Gutierrezia* spp.
Goldenweeds—*Haplopappus* spp.
Paperflower—*Psilotrophe cooperi*
Groundsel—*Senecio* spp.
American trixis—*Trixis californica*

The above listed plants, plus many more in this family and others, come under the field classification of sub- or half-shrubs. This means that the stems are woody at the base, but the upper parts are more herbaceous. This puts them in a class between herbaceous perennials and true shrubs. I have described some of these plants as they occurred in other families for the sake of completeness or because they formed a conspicuous element of the local flora.

The task of describing all these plants is beyond the scope of this book. Since many of the above species of plants bear beautiful or conspicuous flowers, they have been described and pictured in other booklets by Dodge, Patraw, and Arnberger. For this reason, they are omitted here.

Franseria deltoidea, bursage, is a true shrub and occurs abundantly among the paloverde trees of the Arizona and California deserts. It has burr-like fruiting heads with flattened spines. The narrowly triangular leaves are finely toothed and densely covered with short, woolly, matted hairs, on the under surface. The shrubs are between 15 and 30 inches high.

CROWFOOT FAMILY
(Ranunculaceae)

Western Virgins-bower clematis—*Clematis ligusticifolia*
Drummond clematis—*C. drummondii*
"Barbo dechivo"
New Mexico clematis—*C. neomexicana*
Rocky Mountain clematis—*C. pseudoalpina*
Virgins-bower—*C. hirsutissima* var. *schottii*

Although six species of clematis are listed for our area, only the first three are generally considered woody vines, even though the others are woody at the base. *Clematis*, the genus name and the generally used common name, is the Greek name of a

Goldenweed

Western Virgins-bower

climbing vine. *Ligusticifolia* refers to the *Ligusticum*-like leaves; *drummondii* honors Thomas Drummond, an early botanist; *pseudoalpina* means false-alpine to distinguish it from *alpina*, the specific name of a European species; *hirsutissima* refers to hairiness.

Western virgins-bower clematis occurs in moist canyons and in cultivated areas throughout our region. It is frequently seen clinging to fences or growing over trees and shrubs. The opposite, pinnately compound leaves usually have 5 leaflets. They are weakly 3-parted and coarsely serrate. The small, white flowers occur in small clusters. The seeds have long, white tails that give the plant the appearance of being covered with tufts of cotton. It has been used as an ornamental in the West, although more colorful introduced varieties are preferred.

Drummond clematis has much more finely cut leaves than does western virgins-bower clematis. The tails on the seeds are longer and more showy. Its range is also similar but it grows in somewhat drier sites.

New Mexico clematis occurs in southwest New Mexico and southeast Arizona in the higher mountains. Although generally a smaller plant than western virgins-bower clematis, it is so similar botanically that it might be considered a variety of that species.

Rocky Mountain clematis may have violet, purple, or white flowers. It is usually a trailing vine but may be climbing in some circumstances. It occurs in the higher mountains of our area.

Virgins-bower is listed as occurring in Canyonlands National Park.

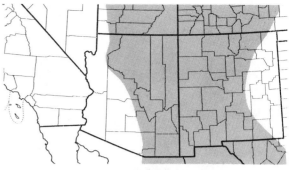

Western Virgins-bower

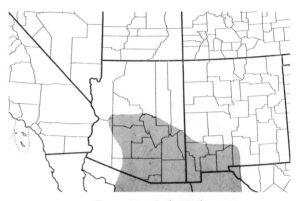

Drummond clematis

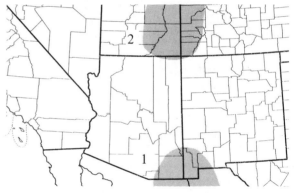

1. New Mexico clematis
2. Virgins-bower

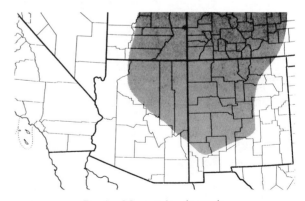

Rocky Mountain clematis

CYPRESS FAMILY
(Cupressaceae)

Arizona cypress—*Cupressus arizonica*
"Cedro, Cedro de la Sierra"
Smooth cypress—*Cupressus glabra*

Cupressus is the name given to Italian cypress, while the specific name honors the state in which it is found. If this tree is found in the wild state in New Mexico at all, it is in the extreme southwest portion, but I have not found it. It is quite common in several areas in southeastern Arizona. I saw a nice stand on Mt. Lemmon north of Tucson at about the 7,000-foot elevation.

The small flowers are borne in the spring. The short-stalked cone is about 1 inch in diameter, made up of hard, gray, woody scales fitted together as a series of small polygons with a point in the center of each. The scale-like leaves are blue-green or yellowish. On the smaller limbs the bark is smooth but shreds with age to expose a dark red inner bark. The wood is lightweight, straight-grained, straw-colored, with a pleasant odor. It is not common enough to be of commercial value. One fine grove is being protected in Chiricahua National Monument.

Some botanists give specific rank to a very similar tree in central Arizona, called smooth cypress, *Cupressus glabra*. It varies from the Arizona cypress in that the bark retains its smooth reddish color into maturity instead of becoming more checked and fissured and darkening in color.

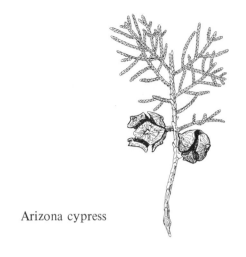

Arizona cypress

1. Smooth cypress
2. Arizona Cypress

Arizona cypress

45

DOGWOOD FAMILY
(Cornaceae)

Wright silktassel—*Garrya wrightii*
Yellow silktassel—*Garrya flavescens*
Goldman silktassel—*Garrya goldmanii*

Wright silktassel

   Garrya honors Nicholas Garry, secretary
of Hudson's Bay Company; *wrightii* honors
Charles Wright, botanist of the Mexican Border Survey; *flavescens* refers to the yellowish
leaves; and *goldmanii* is from a proper name.
   Wright silktassel occurs from west Texas
across southern New Mexico into central
Arizona and south into Mexico. It is found in
the pinon-juniper zone from about 5,000 to
8,000 feet elevation. This is above the zone
where jojoba, a plant with which it might be
confused, is found. It is an evergreen shrub
with several small flowers borne in a cluster
at the ends of the twigs. The seeds are borne
in small, hard, blackish balls from 1/6 to 1/3
inch in diameter. The leaves are up to 2 inches
long, simple, opposite and pointed, and somewhat leathery. The plant normally grows as
a shrub about 6 feet tall but can become treelike in favorable circumstances. Glenn Niner
reports seeing it in the Burro Mountains of
southwest New Mexico, where it was hedged
into a very compact form as a result of deer
browsing, even though it is not generally
considered highly palatable to game or livestock. Wood from old, mature stems is strikingly beautiful. The sapwood is white with
blue shading near the heartwood. The heartwood has various shades of light and dark
brown in an irregularly streaked pattern.
   Yellow silktassel occurs in southeastern
California, eastward into central Arizona,
where it is abundant and north into southern
Utah. The description is about the same as
for Wright silktassel except that the older
leaves are distinctly yellowish.
   Goldman silktassel has been reported
from west Texas into New Mexico.

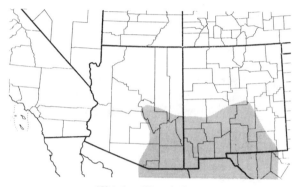

Wright silktassel

Yellow silktassel

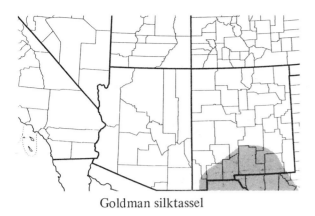

Goldman silktassel

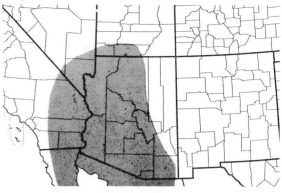

Yellow silktassel

DOGWOOD FAMILY
(Cornaceae)

Redosier dogwood—*Cornus stolonifera*

    Cornus means a horn and refers to the hard wood of dogwood; the species name refers to the habit of the bush to spread by stolons.

    Redosier in our area is a small shrub, spreading or upright, generally under 5 feet tall. The nearly white flowers, borne in May and June, occur in a flat cluster at the ends of the branches. The small fruits, about the size of a kernel of wheat, ripen in the fall. They are whitish to bluish in color. The leaves are opposite with blades narrow and up to 4" long. The twigs are readily noticed, as they are quite red and smooth.

    Redosier is a very widely-spread shrub, occurring across the continent and from New Mexico and Arizona northward to Canada. It prefers moist sites along streams and around swampy or boggy land. It occurs in our mountains to an altitude of about 7,500 feet. It has little wildlife significance.

Redosier dogwood

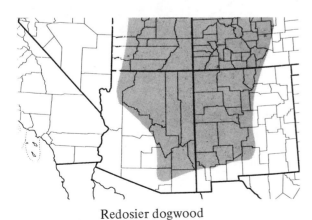

Redosier dogwood

ELM FAMILY
(Ulmaceae)

Netleaf hackberry—*Celtis reticulata*
"Acibuche"

Netleaf hackberry

The naming of the hackberries that may occur in the Southwest is a confusing subject. Some authorities list only *Celtis reticulata* among the trees and *Celtis pallida* as a shrub. Douglas hackberry, *Celtis douglasii*, a hackberry of the Northwest, is listed at Glen Canyon, but one authority lists it also as *C. reticulata.* There is a hackberry in southeastern New Mexico that most resembles *Celtis laevigata* var. *texana* and one in the extreme northeast New Mexico that has wood most like *C. occidentalis.* For various reasons I prefer to consider that there are all five hackberries in the Southwest.

Celtis is the classical Latin name for this genus and *reticulata* refers to the netted leaves, from which it gets its common name. This hackberry occurs as a small tree, up to 30 feet tall and less than 1 foot in diameter, generally. It grows along the dry washes, desert grasslands and river valleys of the southern part of New Mexico, southeastern and central Arizona and on south into Mexico. Its characteristically scraggly appearance develops because several feet of new growth occur on only a few limbs during years of adequate water. The leaves are 1 to 2½ inches long, not symmetrically shaped, dark green, and rough to the touch, like fine sandpaper.

The sweet, one-seeded fruits are orange-red, ¼ to 3/8 inch in diameter. The wood is hard and heavy, cross-grained and hard to work. The color is light gray in the sapwood and mottled gray in the heartwood, flecked with rays.

The largest known hackberry occurs in the Red Rock Wildlife Area of the New Mexico Department of Game and Fish. It measures 11' 4" in circumference, is 74' 2" tall and has a crown spread of 72'. The second largest one is located a few miles up the Gila River in the Gila National Forest.

All the hackberries furnish cover for game and nesting sites for doves and desert songbirds. The fruits are avidly sought by squirrels, songbirds, possibly band-tailed pigeons, and on at least one occasion, by Barbary sheep.

Netleaf hackberry

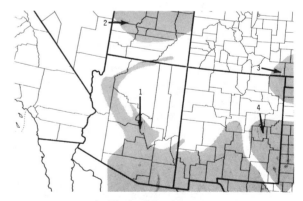

1. Netleaf hackberry
2. Douglas hackberry
3. Common hackberry
4. Sugarberry

ELM FAMILY
(Ulmaceae)

Spiny hackberry—*Celtis pallida*
"Granjeno or Huasteco"

Spiny hackberry

    In the scientific name, *pallida* refers to
the pale branches. This is the smallest of our
hackberries and occurs as a shrub in our area.
It is found in extreme southwest New Mexico
and across southern Arizona, south into
Mexico and east into Texas.
    The small, evergreen leaves are coarsely
toothed or entire, the branches are exceedingly
spiny, and the shrub is densely branched. The
single or paired spines occur closely spaced
along the branches. They are straight, slender,
stiff, and about 1 inch long. The fruit is
bright yellow when ripe and about ¼ inch in
diameter. It is eaten by many species of
desert birds and other wildlife. The wood is
dense and hard, dark straw color streaked
broadly with dark gray to black color. Since
it is small, it has no value as wood. A striking
example of what a good site with plenty of
water will do for a plant was noted in the
Boyce Thompson arboretum. Here I saw a
spiny hackberry nearly 20 feet tall with
branches up to 4 inches in diameter. It bore
fruits profusely.

Spiny hackberry

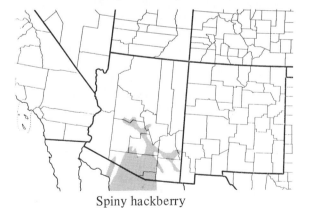
Spiny hackberry

ELM FAMILY
(Ulmaceae)

Common hackberry—*Celtis occidentalis*

    Occidentalis means western, causing one
to wonder how it got applied to the eastern
hackberry. This writer collected wood of a
hackberry at Clayton Lake, north of Clayton,
New Mexico, that appears to be the same as
common hackberry. The species is listed as
growing as far west as western Oklahoma,
where I saw it west of Boise City, so it might
well occur across the line in New Mexico. In
New Mexico these are small, poorly-formed
trees growing in the breaks of the mesa
escarpments where they are protected from
stock. The wood is nearly white with black
imperfections around the knots. It is hard,
heavy, and ring-porous, giving it a course
grain.
    This tree is of too limited occurrence in
our area to be of any importance.

Common hackberry

ELM FAMLY
(Ulmaceae)

Douglas hackberry—*Celtis douglasii*

Douglasii honors David Douglas, an early botanical explorer in the Northwest. This tree is typically found in the Northwest but extends south into Utah and has been listed as occurring in Glen Canyon National Recreation Area. Some authorities prefer to lump Douglas hackberry with netleaf hackberry. However, seen in its native habitat, it appears to be quite different. I saw it on dry hillsides north of Boise, Idaho as a small, poorly-formed tree. The largest one listed from Idaho is only 4' 9" in circumference.

Douglas hackberry

ELM FAMILY
(Ulmaceae)

Sugarberry—*Celtis laevigata* var. *texana*

Laevigata means smooth, but why the word was chosen is not known. This hackberry, or sugarberry as it is called, is a tree of west Texas, extending on west to the area around Fort Sumner, New Mexico. Here on the high plains it grows in sheltered arroyos and hollows where it is seldom seen except by the local ranchers.

The tree grows to 6 to 8 inches in diameter and about 30 feet tall or larger. It presents a less scraggly appearance than netleaf hackberry. The berries are dark red or purple when ripe.

The color of the wood of sugarberry lacks the grayness characteristic of netleaf hackberry but is not as white as common hackberry. Otherwise, its characteristics are similar. The tree is not of general enough occurrence to be of any value except for food and cover for local wildlife.

Sugarberry

ELM FAMILY
(Ulmaceae)

Siberian elm—*Ulmus pumila*

Many trees have been introduced into the Southwest from other States and foreign countries, mostly as shade or ornamentals. Many kinds are not sufficiently hardy to reproduce from seed and spread to new areas. However, there are several notable exceptions and Siberian elm is one of the most prominent. Siberian elm seeds prolifically. Wild, self-planted seedlings have become established and have grown to trees without any care or attention from man; thus, they may be considered naturalized.

In the scientific name *Ulmus* is the Latin word for elm and *pumila* means dwarf. There has been considerable confusion about the correct name for this introduced elm. The *Woody Plant Seed Manual* of the Forest Service states that the elm which ripens its seed in the spring is properly called Siberian elm, *Ulmus pumila*, but lists Chinese elm as a synonym. Chinese elm is properly *Ulmus parvifolia*, and it ripens seed in August and September.

Siberian elm has been used extensively in the Southwest for shade tree planting in towns and villages and for shelter from the wind and has become established as a naturalized tree. It is a medium-sized tree with a broadly spreading crown. The leaves are about 1 inch broad and 2 inches long with serrated edges. The flowers are small, but the large number borne gives the tree a mauve to brown color early in the spring before the leaves appear. The numerous fruits form drifts along the streets of the towns as they fall. No distribution map is needed, as this tree has been introduced in towns and around homesteads throughout our area.

From a wildlife standpoint, these trees furnish cover for all types of animals and nest sites for tree-nesting birds. The leaves are palatable to deer, and this may tend to keep them from becoming established very widely in deer range. The wood is darker brown and has a more distinct figure to the grain than American elm, but it is brash and structurally weak. It would make attractive veneer if it could be harvested in commercial quantities.

There are no elms native to the Southwest.

Siberian elm

EPHEDRA FAMILY
(Ephedraceae)

Mormontea—*Ephedra viridis*
Desert jointfir or ephedra—*E. trifurca*
"Colorin" or "Coralina"
Nevada jointfir or ephedra—*E. nevadensis*
Torrey jointfir or ephedra—*E. torreyana*
Erect jointfir or ephedra—*E. antisyphilitica*
"Canitilla"
Rough ephedra—*E. nevadensis* var. *aspera*

Ephedra is the ancient Greek name. *Viridis* refers to the green stems; *trifurca* refers to the 3-forked branches and leaves; *torreyana* honors John Torrey, an American botanist; *antisyphilitica* refers to the use of this plant in the treatment of syphilis, although other species have also been used; and *aspera* refers to the roughness of the stems.

The common name for these plants is confusing. The name "mormontea" is often loosely applied to all of them in the field but should properly be reserved for *E. viridis*. Also, some writers have tried to standardize with the name jointfir, whereas others have tried to establish the generic name as the common name.

The mormontea, as here used, occurs in northwestern New Mexico north into Colorado and westward through Arizona and Utah to California. It is generally found in sandy places or on rocky slopes, as a shrub up to 4 feet high. It is much branched and broomlike with very tiny leaves, awl-shaped and clustered around the joints of the stems, which are green in color. The tiny, greenish or yellow flowers also occur at the joints. The plant has been used medicinally, as have most of the species of the genus, and as a substitute for tea.

Desert jointfir occurs in the Lower Sonoran Zone in the dry hills to 6,000 feet in New Mexico, western Texas, Arizona to California and south into Mexico. It often becomes a larger shrub, to 6 feet tall, and with a larger stem than mormontea. Otherwise it is similar in appearance, except that the leaves are longer, united at the base around the stem joints, and are three-parted. The stems are somewhat three-forked, and may have weak spines at the tips. The larger stems are usually involuted and so rotten they cannot be used for anything.

The other jointfirs are quite similar to the ones described, and their ranges are largely overlapping so that it will be difficult to distinguish which species is being observed.

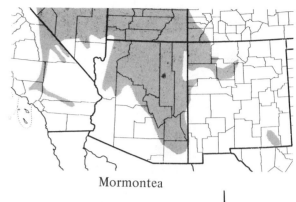

Mormontea

Desert jointfir

Desert jointfir

All of the jointfirs have some value for grazing, especially as an emergency winter food for cattle, sheep and mule deer. They serve as an erosion control plant and provide cover for small mammals and birds. The brown, nut-like seeds are edible roasted, and are also taken by quail and other birds.

Some botanists consider that it is improper to apply the word "flower" to the male and female organs of gymnosperms. However, I have chosen to follow the lead of Little, Vines, and many others who use the term.

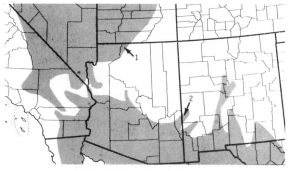

1. Nevada jointfir
2. Desert jointfir

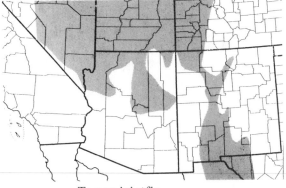

Torrey jointfir

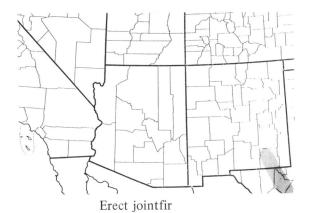

Erect jointfir

Rough ephedra

GOOSEFOOT FAMILY
(Chenopodiaceae)

Fourwing saltbush—*Atriplex canescens*
Shadscale—*Atriplex confertifolia*
Big saltbush—*Atriplex lentiformis*
"Chamiso, Cenizo"

Fourwing saltbush

Atriplex is the classical name of the genus; *canescens* refers to the gray or silvery pubescence on the leaves; *confertifolia* refers to the crowded leaves; and *lentiformis* refers to the lenslike fruits. Several species of *Atriplex* are reported from various parts of our area, but the three named are the important shrub forms. At least some of the others should be classed as sub-shrubs.

Fourwing saltbush is said to be the most widely spread species of *Atriplex* in the United States. It occurs in suitable sites throughout our area. The erect, evergreen shrub grows to a height of 8 feet but more generally about 4 feet in height. The female bushes are readily recognized, as they bear the fruits. The seed is small and burrlike, but it is surrounded by 4 papery winglike bracts, very light brown to whitish in color, and about ½ inch across. The small, narrow alternate leaves are gray in color due to the dense scurf on both sides. The stems are small, but the sapwood is light green, and the heart is nearly white. This saltbush occurs throughout our area and no map of distribution is needed.

Shadscale is generally a shorter shrub than fourwing or big saltbush. The fruiting bodies have 2 wings instead of 4. The small, grayish green deciduous leaves are rounded and, as they fall, reveal short spines on the stiff branches. Shadscale is found in alkaline localities over most of our area.

Big saltbush is as large as fourwing but appears to be more sparsely branched. The small, more or less heart-shaped, scurfy, silvery leaves are persistent in moist situations but soon drop off in desert situations. The tiny seeds occur in long drooping spikes at the ends of the branches. This plant occurs sparsely over much of our area.

The various species of *Atriplex* are highly valuable as forage for domestic stock on the range, which graze the leaves and stems and eat the seeds. They are also utilized by deer, antelope, and Barbary sheep for feed and cover. They also serve to protect the soil from erosion and furnish cover for many types of desert birds and mammals.

Fourwing saltbush

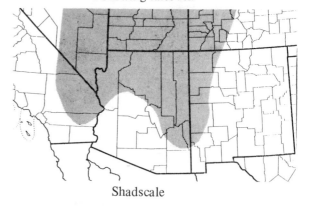
Shadscale

Big saltbush

54

GOOSEFOOT FAMILY
(Chenopodiaceae)

Winterfat—*Eurotia lanata*

Eurotia is from *euros*, Greek for mould, referring to the mouldy appearance of the leaves. *Lanata* comes from the Latin *lana*, meaning wool or hair, and refers to the woolly appearance of the seeding stalks of the plant.

Winterfat is a low-growing half-shrub that occurs widely spread in our area except for southwest Arizona. Since the plant is woody only at the base, a description of it may not belong in this book, but it is so conspicuous it is well worth mentioning.

Under heavy grazing pressure, it may seldom be over about 8 inches tall but in better sites reaches 3 feet in height. The small, narrow leaves are alternate or clustered along the stem and are densely hairy, giving it a gray appearance. The fluffy seeds are borne along the upper third of the stem, giving the plant a white or silvery appearance. The base of the stem is woody.

The plant is heavily used by domestic stock and receives some use by game, but feeding trials have shown it not to be a preferred deer feed in New Mexico. Desert bighorn sheep, antelope, and Barbary sheep have been known to utilize it.

No distribution map is needed, as this plant occurs throughout our area except in southwest Arizona and southeast California.

Winterfat

Winterfat

GOOSEFOOT FAMILY
(Chenopodiaceae)

Spiny hop sage—*Grayia spinosa*
Spineless hop sage—*Grayia brandegi*

The genus name honors Asa Gray, early leader in American systematic botany, *spinosa* refers to the spiny nature of the plant, and *brandegi* honors a man.

Spiny hop sage is limited to the Mohave Desert part of our area in southwestern Utah, southern Nevada, extreme northwest Arizona and west into California. It occurs in the sagebrush and creosotebush desert lands between 2,500 and 7,000 feet elevation as a shrub up to about 3 feet in height. It is similar to the saltbushes, but the bracts surrounding the fruit are almost completely united, except at the top, to form a sack. The somewhat scurfy leaves are about one inch long, narrow, and somewhat fleshy. The female flowers are borne in spikes. The branches form spines when the leaves fall.

This is a valuable forage plant in the desert, where it grows in abundance.

Another species, spineless hop sage, has been reported from the Petrified Forest National Park in northeast Arizona and from areas in southeast Utah.

GOOSEFOOT FAMILY
(Chenopodiaceae)

Black greasewood—*Sarcobatus vermiculatus*

Sarcobatus is made up of two words; *sarco* means fleshy and *batus* is Greek for bramble bush; thus, the bramble plant with fleshy leaves. *Vermiculatus* refers to the wormy appearance of the embryo.

Greasewood is widely spread over our area, and occurs locally on seepy, alkaline soils. Here it grows as a shrub generally about 6 feet tall but may grow to 10 feet in favorable sites. The alternate leaves are long and narrow and nearly round in cross section, with a fleshy appearance, pale green or gray in color. The male and female flowers are borne in separate parts of the same plant. The female flowers are borne in the axils of the leaves and are not conspicuous. The male flowers are borne in terminal clusters on the twigs and appear as small conelike structures. The weakly spiny twigs may grow to about 3 inches in diameter, but they are so involuted

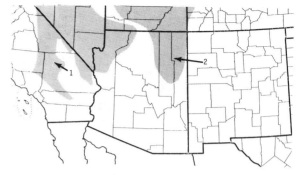

1. Spiny hop sage
2. Spineless hop sage

Black greasewood

Black greasewood

that it is hard to find a solid piece of wood.
It is heavy, hard, and light tan in color.

Greasewood draws the soil salts in
solution into the leaves. As the leaves fall to
the ground and rot, the salt remains on the
soil surface. Many unwary settlers learned to
their dismay that such soil was very difficult
to make productive. The spot where a greasewood plant stood in a field shows as a bare
area for many years.

The plant serves as reserve forage for
livestock and is utilized by game to some
extent as cover and by prairie dogs for food.

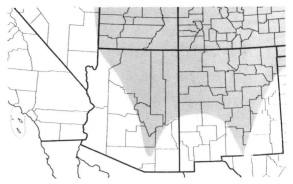

Black greasewood

Fiveleaf ivy

GRAPE FAMILY
(Vitaceae)

Fiveleaf ivy or thicket creeper—
Parthenocissus vitacea

The scientific name is sometimes given
as *P. inserta*. Another common name is
thicket creeper and is sometimes wrongly
referred to as woodbine. The genus name
comes from Greek *parthenos*, meaning virgin,
and *kissos* for ivy. *Vitacea* has reference to
the grapelike tendrils. Fiveleaf ivy is often
called Virginia creeper, a name more properly applied to a very similar species
occurring from Texas eastward. The plant
is of widespread occurrence, extending from
Texas and New Mexico northeast to Nova
Scotia. It has been used widely as an ornamental. It climbs freely over fences and
into trees. The 5-lobed leaves turn bright
red in fall along with the ripening of the
numerous deep purplish-black berries. The
fruits are avidly sought by various species
of birds. The 5-lobed leaves plainly distinguish this plant from poison ivy, a plant
with 3-lobed leaves, and not a vine in our
area.

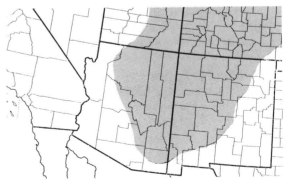

Fiveleaf ivy

GRAPE FAMILY
(Vitaceae)

Canyon grape—*Vitis arizonica*
"Vid" or "para"
Frost grape—*Vitis vulpina*

Vitis is the classical Latin name for the genus. *Vulpina* refers to the fox, which avidly eats the fruits.

Canyon grape occurs in west Texas, southern New Mexico, and in central Arizona. It reaches its best development in southwestern New Mexico. A vine near the Gila Cliff Dwellings National Monument has a main stem 1 foot in diameter. Vines with 6-inch stems are fairly common and the vines literally cover the trees over which they are growing. Grapes are readily recognized by the generally 3-pointed, serrate leaves, the tendrils, the climbing habit of growth, and in season by the clusters of black, sweet grapes. In areas where grapes bear heavily, local families have the individual vines located and resent newcomers' picking the fruit from them. The fruit is highly prized for jellies and preserves.

The range for frost grape is given as New Mexico and eastward. The leaves are less strongly 3-lobed than in canyon grape. Otherwise, the plants are quite similar.

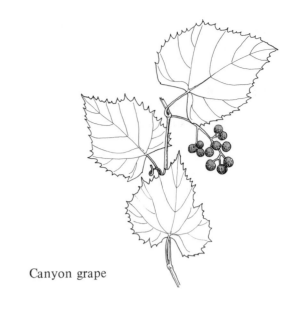

Canyon grape

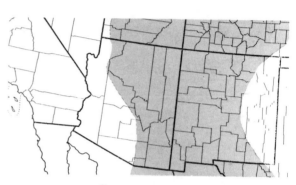

Canyon grape

HEATH FAMILY
(Ericaceae)

Point-leaf manzanita—*Arctostaphylos pungens*
"Manzanita" or "Pinguica"
Green-leaf manzanita—*A. patula*
Pringle manzanita—*A. pringlei*
Bearberry or Kinnikinnick—*A. uva-ursi*

In the genus name *Arcto* means bear and *staphylos* a grape cluster, thus literally bearberry. *Pungens* means pointed, *patula* refers to the spreading growth habit, and *pringlei* honors a man. *Uva-ursi* again means bearberry, a unique combination of the common name, genus name, and specific name, all meaning the same thing.

The manzanitas are readily distinguished by their low, spreading growth habit in our area, and the smooth red bark and crooked, twisted limbs. Point-leaf manzanita is the manzanita of the southern mountains, north

Point-leaf manzanita

58

to the central part of New Mexico and Arizona. It occurs on dry gravelly hillsides in the ponderosa pine forest zone. The leaves are about twice as long as they are broad and pointed at tip and base. The small, nodding, pink or white flowers are borne at the tips of the branches. The small fruits are dark brown or reddish with several seeds and soft pulp. The wood is hard and heavy. The thin sapwood is light brown and the heart is deep reddish brown, flecked with red rays.

Green-leaf manzanita is the manzanita of the northern part of our area, occurring in southern Utah, Colorado, northern Arizona, and California. It is distinguished by its nearly round leaves. Fine specimens may be seen in Utah along Highway 89 near Long Valley Junction.

Pringle manzanita occurs in southeastern Arizona, where it grows to 6 feet tall. The leaves are more rounded at the base than those in point-leaf manzanita.

Bearberry is a very widely spread shrub encircling the northern hemisphere. In our area it occurs in the high mountains as a very low-growing, spreading shrub in the mixed conifer and spruce zones. The nodding flowers are white or pink and the berries red. The leaves are small and rounded.

Where the manzanitas grow in dense clumps over large areas they are a problem to range managers, as they are not valuable as forage plants and the thick mat prevents more useful plants from growing. They are browsed lightly by big game animals and the seeds are sought by forest-dwelling grouse and other birds. The chief value is as ground cover to prevent erosion.

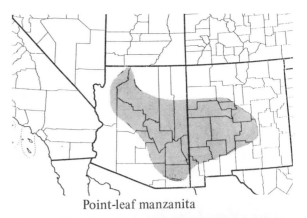

Point-leaf manzanita

Point-leaf manzanita

Bearberry

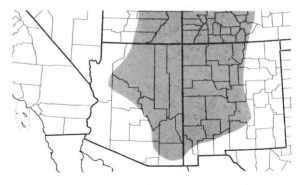

Bearberry or Kinnikinnick
(high mountains)

Green-leaf manzanita

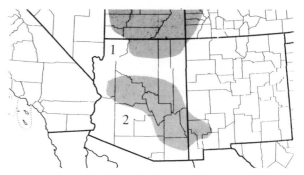

1. Green-leaf manzanita
2. Pringle manzanita

HEATH FAMILY
(Ericaceae)

Grouse whortleberry—*Vaccinium scoparium*

Vaccinium is thought to be from the
Latin *vaccinus*, of cows; *scoparium* refers to
the broomlike branches.

Grouse whortleberry grows in the highest
mountains of our area from New Mexico to
California and northward. It is a very low-
growing plant, seldom over 1 foot tall, found
in the mixed conifer and spruce zones, where
it makes excellent ground cover. The tiny
white flowers occur in the axils of the leaves.
The dark red or wine-colored berries are sweet
and edible. The leaves are only slightly over
½ inch long. This plant occurs in the same
range as bearberry but can be distinguished
by the very small leaves, the sweet berries,
and the fact that the flowers are borne singly
rather than in small bunches. Wildlife
utilize the berries and also browse the plants
to some extent.

Whortleberry and bearberry both exhibit
a growth habit common to many high altitude
plants in that they are low-growing or creeping. Even the spruce trees take on this
growth form at timberline. This is related to
the harsh environment. Heavy snows come
early in the autumn and last into early
summer. This literally crushes the shrubs to
the ground. It also makes the growing season
very short. During the winter the low temp-
eratures tend to kill back growth that is not
protected by snow, and at timberline the high
winds, driving ice and sleet scour off the
branches on the windward side and at the top.
Other shrubs that exhibit this environmental
response are creeping mahonia, common juniper, shrubby cinquefoil to some extent,
myrtle-boxleaf, mountain ninebark, summit
willow, and bearberry.

Grouse whortleberry

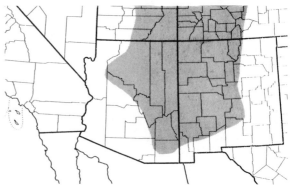

Grouse whortleberry
(high mountains)

60

HEATH FAMILY
(Ericaceae)

Arizona madrone—*Arbutus arizonica*
"Madrono"
Texas madrone—*Arbutus texana*

Arizona madrone

Arbutus is the classical name for the south European genus. The specific names are for the States where they were found.

Arizona madrone is listed as occurring in extreme southwestern New Mexico and southeastern Arizona, south into Mexico. I found good specimens in the Chiricahua Mountains of southeastern Arizona in the canyon above Portal. Here it reaches a height of about 30 feet and a diameter up to 2 feet. Since the ranges of our two species are so widely separated, there will be no confusion in identification. The leaves of Arizona madrone are long and slender with conspicuous red stems and midrib. The fruit, borne terminally, is a small ball with rough outer coating, dark reddish brown. The young twigs are bright red with scaly bark on the older twigs. The bark of the trunk is grayish brown, divided into squares and separated into vertical ridges. It does not appear to peel off and reveal smooth underbark as does Texas madrone. The wood is quite hard and heavy with straw-colored sapwood and pinkish-brown heart.

Texas madrone occurs in west Texas, the Guadalupe Mountains of New Mexico, and south into Mexico. A nice small grove may be seen in Guadalupe Mountain National Park where Highway U.S. 180 crosses the corner of the park near Pine Springs about 60 miles southwest of Carlsbad, New Mexico. Botanically the tree is similar to Arizona madrone except that the bark on older trunks peels off, revealing patches of smooth reddish-brown underlayer, the berries are larger and bright red and the stems and veins of the leaves are not red in older trees. The wood is similar to Arizona madrone. All madrone is hard to cure, as it checks very badly.

The fruit of madrone is utilized by various species of birds and the leaves furnish limited forage for mule deer. Otherwise, they are not common enough to be of value.

Arizona madrone

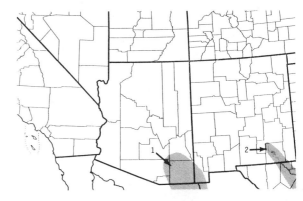

1. Arizona madrone
2. Texas madrone

Texas madrone

Texas madrone

Texas madrone

HONEYSUCKLE FAMILY
(Caprifoliaceae)

Twinberry honeysuckle—*Lonicera involu-*
crata
Hairy white honeysuckle—*L. albiflora* var.
dumosa
Arizona honeysuckle—*L. arizonica*
Utah honeysuckle—*L. utahensis*
Chaparral honeysuckle—*L. interrupta*

   Lonicera honors Adam Lonitzer, a German botanist; *involucrata* refers to the long involucral bracts; *albiflora* refers to white flowers; and *dumosa* is from a Latin noun meaning bramble.

   Twinberry honeysuckle gets its common name from the fact that the flowers, and later the berries, are borne in pairs. They occur in the leaf axils and are almost obscured by the large involucral bracts, from which it gets the scientific name. Another common name is bearberry honeysuckle. It occurs high in the Sangre de Cristo Mountains of New Mexico and northward. It grows as a tall shrub, almost vinelike at times, in thickets or singly. The involucral bracts turn red as the berries ripen and turn black. The leaves are opposite, deciduous, and up to 5 inches long.

   Hairy white honeysuckle is a variety of white honeysuckle with hairy stems and leaves. White honeysuckle bears its flowers in terminal clusters and is a shrub or partly climbing vine to 9 feet tall that occurs in southern New Mexico and Arizona. The variety occurs in the Chiricahua Mountains of southeastern Arizona.

   Arizona honeysuckle is said to range through west Texas, New Mexico, and Arizona, and south into Mexico. The flowers, borne in small terminal clusters, have red corolla tubes. The ripe berries are red. The plant is usually a stiff, trailing vine.

   Utah honeysuckle occurs in the high mountains from 8,000 to 10,000 feet in New Mexico and through Arizona to California. It is also a twinberry honeysuckle with flowers borne in the axils of the leaves.

   Chaparral honeysuckle occurs in Gila and Pima Counties in Arizona.

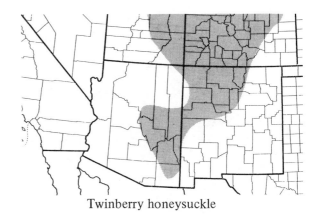

Twinberry honeysuckle

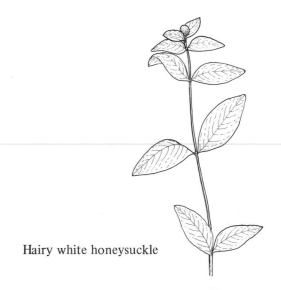

Hairy white honeysuckle

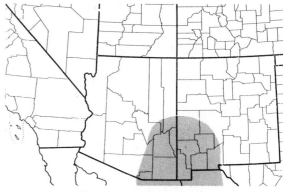

Hairy white honeysuckle

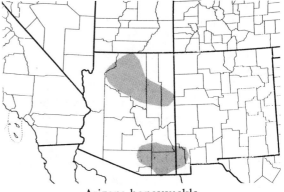

Arizona honeysuckle

63

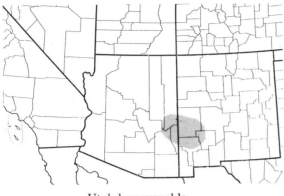

Utah honeysuckle
(also listed for Utah)

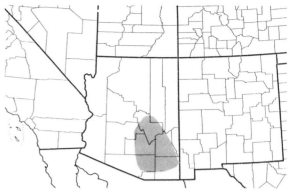

Chaparral honeysuckle

Mexican elder

Mexican elder
(leaf and fruit detail)

HONEYSUCKLE FAMILY
(*Caprifoliaceae*)

Mexican elder—*Sambucus mexicana*
"Sauco"
Blueberry elder—*Sambucus glauca*
"Sauco"
Scarlet elder—*Sambucus pubens*
Blackbead elder—*Sambucus melanocarpa*
Velvet elder—*Sambucus glauca,* var. *velutina*

    Sambucus is the classical Latin name for
the genus. *Mexicana* is the Latinized form of
Mexico, *glauca* refers to the bloom on the ripe
fruit, *pubens* to the pubescent growth sometimes found on young growth, and *melano-
carpa* literally means black fruit. *Velutina*
refers to the dense undercovering of hairs.
    Mexican elder occurs in the Rio Grande and
Gila drainages in New Mexico and in the
southern and central parts of Arizona along
streams and drainages in the desert and desert
grassland. An evergreen, it has been used as an
ornamental from Albuquerque southward.
It is hard to distinguish from blueberry elder
except that the berries are black. It tends to
grow in clumps and will develop to a tree
about 20 feet tall and up to a foot in diameter. The wood is soft and lightweight with
a soft pith. It is hard to cure, as it warps and
checks badly.
    The berries are utilized by wildlife and are
also gathered locally for use in pies and jelly.
This can also be said for the other elders.
    Blueberry elder occurs higher in the moun-
tains in the ponderosa pine zone and upward,
where it makes a large shrub or small tree,
generally in clumps. It may be distinguished
from Mexican elder by the altitudinal range
of its habitat and by the fact that it usually
has 5 to 6 leaflets per compound leaf rather
than 3 to 5 found in the Mexican elder. The
wood is lightweight, soft with a large soft pith,

light brown color. *S. neomexicana* is a
synonym for *S. glauca.*

Velvet elder is reported from the Hualpai
Mountains and on west into California. The
undersurface of the leaves is finely and densely
densely hairy.

Blackbead and scarlet elder are both shrub
forms that occur high in the conifer belt on
the high mountains of our region. The blackbead elder may be distinguished in fruiting
by its black fruits, contrasted with the orange
to red fruits of scarlet elder. The range of
blackbead elder is listed as New Mexico westward to California and for scarlet elder as
from New Mexico eastward. The main dist-
inction is in the color of the fruits. Scarlet
elder closely resembles European red elder,
S. racemosa. Some writers believe it to be
the same. *S. microbotrys* may be a variety
of *S. racemosa.*

In all the elders, the flowers and later the
very small berries occur in large, more or less
flat-topped to rounded clusters, 8 to 10 inches
in diameter. The leaves are paired and
pinnately compound with 3 to 9 large,
pointed, serrated leaflets to a stem. The
elders are avidly sought after by birds in berry
season.

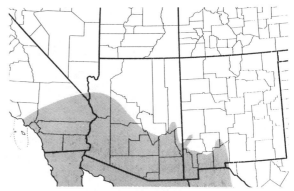
Mexican elder

Blueberry elder

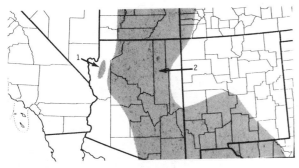
1. Velvet elder
2. Blueberry elder

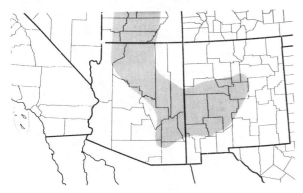
Blackbead elder

Blueberry elder

65

Scarlet elder

Scarlet elder
(flower and leaf detail)

HONEYSUCKLE FAMILY
(Caprifoliaceae)

Mountain snowberry
Symphoricarpos oreophilus
Common snowberry
Symphoricarpos albus
Palmer snowberry
Symphoricarpos palmeri
Roundleaf snowberry
Symphoricarpos rotundifolius
Western snowberry
Symphoricarpos longiflorus

The genus name comes from the Greek *sympherein*, to bear together, and *karpos*, fruit, referring to the clustered fruits. *Oreophilus* means mountain-loving, *albus* refers to the white berries, *palmeri* honors Ernest Jesse Palmer, *rotundifolius* refers to the round leaves, *longiflorus* refers to the long-tubed corolla, and *pauciflorus* refers to small flowers

The snowberries commonly occur in the ponderosa pine zone in our area. They are low, spreading, or upright shrubs, deciduous, and often locally abundant, growing in thick stands. They are characterized by small pink or rose flowers with long corollas, borne in the axils of the opposite leaves. The fruit is small and snow-white when ripe. The leaves are small, the older twigs are brown and shreddy. The plants vary as to palatability by species and by area, but most species are considered important to domestic stock and mule

Mountain snowberry

Mountain snowberry

66

deer. They also serve an important role in
furnishing ground cover to prevent erosion.

Mountain snowberry has rose-colored
flowers; the others are pink. Palmer snowberry is often more trailing, with branches to
6 feet long. Roundleaf snowberry, as the
name implies, has rounded leaves up to 1½
inches long. Western snowberry flowers have
corollas up to ½ inch long, which is long for
snowberries.

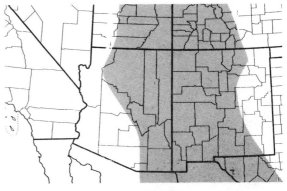

Mountain snowberry

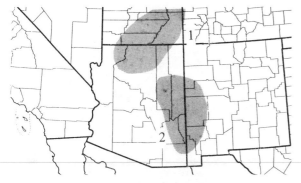

1. Common snowberry
2. Palmer snowberry

Common snowberry

Palmer snowberry

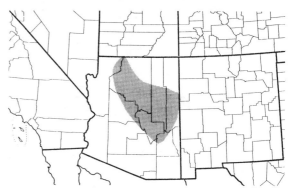

Roundleaf snowberry

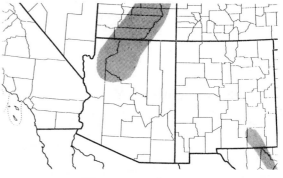

Western snowberry

67

LEGUME FAMILY
(Leguminosae)

Catclaw acacia—*Acacia greggii*
"Una de gato"
Mescat acacia or whitethorn—*A. constricta*
"Largoncillo"
Viscid acacia—*Acacia vernicosa*
Sweet acacia—*Acacia farnesiana*
"Huisache" or "Binorama"
Roemer acacia—*Acacia roemeriana*
Santa Rita acacia—*Acacia millefolia*
Fern acacia—*Acacia angustissima*
"Timbe"

Catclaw acacia

Acacia is from an old word meaning hard, sharp point. The specific names *greggii, farnesiana* and *roemeriana* honor men. *Constricta* refers to the constrictions between the seeds in the pods, *vernicosa* means shiny, *angustissima* refers to the very narrow leaflets, and *millefolia* may refer to the hundreds of minute leaflets into which each leaf is divided.

Two other species, *A. angustifolia* and *A. emoriana*, are reported from Carlsbad National Park.

The acacias are an important component of the thorn forest of Mexico that extends northward into New Mexico and Arizona to varying degrees. Perhaps the most conspicuous species is catclaw acacia. It occurs in the Lower Sonoran Zone of New Mexico, across the same zone in Arizona, and west into southern California. It will be easily recognized and not soon forgotten if a person gets too close to it, as the spines along the branches are curved back like the claws of a cat. It might be confused with catclaw mimosa, which has similar spines, except that the flowers are cylindrical and yellow rather than globular and pink to white, and the leaves are composed of few leaflets rather than many as in the catclaw mimosa. The rather persistent pods are up to 5 inches long, ½ inch wide, and somewhat constricted. The wood is strong, hard, and heavy, used locally for handles, trinkets and fuel. It has white sapwood and deep red heartwood. The largest known tree occurs in the exotic-game pasture of the Department of Game and Fish at Red Rock, New Mexico. It measures 6 feet 5 inches in circumference and 49 feet 4 inches in height, with a crown spread of 46 feet.

Mescat acacia or whitethorn is common in the Lower Sonoran Zone of our area and south into Texas and Mexico. This is a shrub, usually 6 to 8 feet tall, that may reach heights of up to 18 feet. It occurs on dry, sandy or limestone soils up to an elevation of

Catclaw acacia (with Western honey mesquite)

The largest catclaw acacia

68

6,000 feet. The main leaf stem is up to 2 inches long with 3 to 7 secondary leaf stems, each with 6 to 16 pairs of tiny leaflets. The small, globular, yellow flowers are borne in the leaf axils in pairs or more, on stalks up to 1 inch long or longer. The long, slender, reddish brown to black seed pods are up to 4 inches long and somewhat constricted between the beans. The stems are armed with pairs of straight spines set at the base of the leaf stalk. They may be white, grayish, or brown and from ¼ to 1 inch long. The stems are not large but the heartwood is very red and the sapwood is white. The wood is hard and heavy.

Viscid acacia occurs sparsely and scattered in southeastern Arizona and more abundantly in the Lower Sonoran Zone in New Mexico on gravelly or limestone hillsides. It has 2 to 4 pairs of primary leaflets with 5 to 7 secondary leaflets to a stem. The small, yellow flowers are crowded into small ball-shaped heads on short stalks attached to the twigs at the axils of the leaves. Here also are attached a pair of gray or white spines up to 1 inch long. The open-growing shrubs reach a height of about 6 feet and are sticky.

Sweet acacia occurs only in two mountain ranges in southern Arizona and locally in southern California, but is more common in Mexico and southward. It becomes a tree but otherwise is similar in characteristics to Mescat acacia, except that the pods are cylindrical.

The other acacias are less important. Roemer acacia has white to pale green flowers clustered to small balls. The flowers of Santa Rita acacia are white and crowded into cylindrical spikes up to 1 inch long. Fern acacia has white to lavender flowers crowded into balls about ½ inch in diameter.

The acacias have some value as forage for livestock and the seeds are taken by quail and other desert birds. The plants furnish the cover and shade so badly needed on the desert.

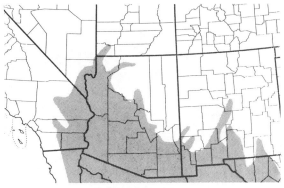

Catclaw acacia

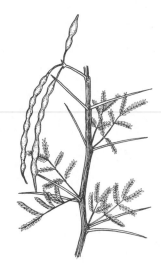

Whitethorn
Mescat acacia

Whitethorn

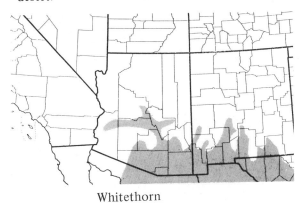

Whitethorn

69

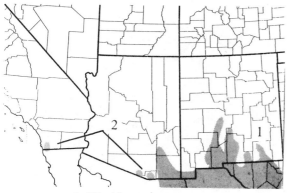

1. Viscid acacia
2. Sweet acacia (also in Mexico)

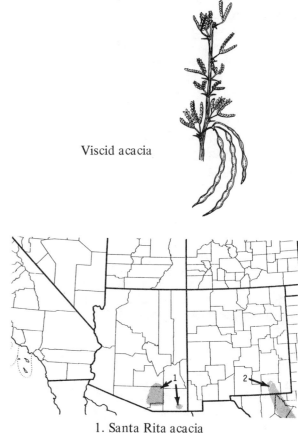

Viscid acacia

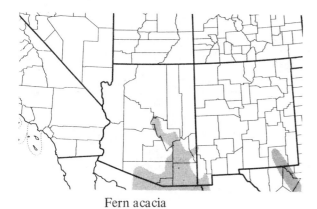

Fern acacia

1. Santa Rita acacia
2. Roemer acacia

LEGUME FAMILY
(Leguminosae)

Smoketree—*Dalea spinosa*
"Corona-de-Cristo"
Indigo bush—*Dalea fremontii*
Feather dalea—*Dalea formosa*

    Dalea honors Samuel Dale, English bot-
anist. *Spinosa* refers to spiny; *fremontii*
honors General Charles Fremont, early
explorer of the West; and *formosa* has reference to the pretty flowers. Many other
species of *Dalea* occur in our area, but these
three are representative of the treelike or
shrubby ones.
    Smoketree, or smokethorn dalea as it is
called by some writers, is the best known of
the daleas. It occurs in the Sonoran Desert
area of extreme western Arizona, up the Colorado drainage to Gila Bend and in southeastern
California. It is found in the dry washes, where
it receives extra moisture. It is said that the
seeds are so hard they require scarification by
being tumbled among the rocks and gravel of

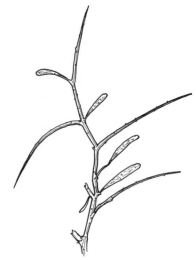

Smoketree

the dry wash before they will germinate. The plant occurs as a shrub or small tree up to about about 25 feet tall. The leaves are few and simple but fall off quickly as dry weather begins. The small, pea-like deep blue to purple flowers occur in clusters at the ends of the spiny branches. The whole tree, when not in bloom, has an ashy gray color so it is not hard to think of it as resembling a puff of smoke in the arroyo. In order to give protection to these rare and interesting trees it is now illegal to cut them. I have seen a specimen of the wood which showed white sapwood and light brown heartwood streaked with darker pores. The wood was moderately hard and heavy.

Indigo bush is listed under several variety names, each with rather specific geographical orientation. It seems sufficient for our purposes to list only the species name. The name is applied rather loosely to any of several blue-flowered legumes. The indigo bush of western Arizona and southeastern California grows in much the same habitat as the smoke tree but is not so closely tied to the arroyos or dry washes. It is frequently found on the small ridges between the dry washes in southeastern California in and around the desert. The plant is shrubby to about 8 feet in height, densely branched, spiny, with enlarged nodes. The general color is ashy gray, like smoketree, but not so pronounced. The small leaves are generally absent but the deep blue, pea-like flowers are spectacular in season.

Feather dalea has a much wider distribution in our area. It is found in west Texas, across southern New Mexico, up the Rio Grande drainage to Albuquerque, and westward in southeastern Arizona, northwest across the center toward Kingman. It is representative of the small, low-growing shrub daleas. It may be nearly prostrate or upright to about 3 feet in height. The small, bicompound leaves give a feathery appearance to the plant. The small, blue, pea-like flowers are pretty but not spectacular like those of indigo bush.

The daleas are of little importance to livestock but are utilized by deer for food and no doubt the seeds are eaten by birds and rodents. The plants provide some cover and help to bind the soil and slow down runoff of the rainfall.

Smoketree

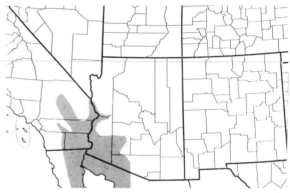

Smoketree

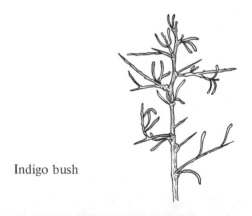

Indigo bush

Indigo bush 71

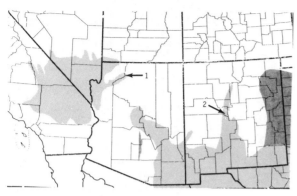

1. Indigo bush
2. Feather dalea

Feather dalea

Feather dalea (flower detail)

LEGUME FAMILY
(Leguminosae)

Yellow or foothills paloverde—
    Cercidium microphyllum
Blue paloverde—*C. floridum*
Mexican paloverde, horse bean, or
Jerusalem thorn—*Parkinsonia aculeata*
"Retama"
"Palo verde"

    Two genera are considered together here
as they are so similar and occur, in part, in the
same area. *Cercidium* is from a Greek word,
Kerkidion, meaning a weaver's comb, supposedly
referring to the pod. *Microphyllum* means
little leaf, and *floridum* refers to the abundance
of flowers in this desert plant. *Parkinsonia*
honors John Parkinson, English botanist,
and *aculeata* refers to the spine on the stems.
    Yellow or foothills paloverde is found
in the Sonoran desert of Arizona and south
into Mexico from Tucson and near Benson,
westward to the Colorado River and across
into California in the Whipple Mountains

Yellow paloverde

south of Needles. It does not occur in New Mexico. Paloverde means green pole in Spanish and all three of our species fulfill this description. Yellow paloverde may be said to be yellowish-green, while blue paloverde is more bluish green, but these are not reliable diagnostic characteristics. In yellow paloverde the small leaflets are arranged in pairs along a rachis about 6 to 8 inches long. The showy yellow flowers, about 1 inch across, have a light cream or white banner. The pods are short and tightly constricted between the beans, of which there are usually 2 to 4. The tree is many-branched, up to about 1 foot in diameter and 15 or more feet in height. The wood is pale yellow, quite soft, and is much easier to cure than blue paloverde.

Blue paloverde is readily distinguished from yellow paloverde when leaflets are present as they are borne on a short rachis with 2 to 3 pairs of leaflets per rachis. The flowers are bright yellow, including the banner, and the pods are not tightly constricted between between the seeds. The tree is more apt to be found in the valleys and along the dry washes rather than on the foothills, the habitat of the yellow paloverde. Blue paloverde may grow somewhat larger but seldom as high as 20 feet or more than 1 foot in diameter. It occurs from just west of the New Mexico border with Arizona on the Gila River, all across southern Arizona and over the Sonoran desert area of southeastern California, south into Baja California and Mexico. The wood is very similar to that of yellow paloverde. Blue paloverde is the state tree of Arizona.

Mexican paloverde is, of course, more prevalent in Mexico but does occur within our area. It grows near El Centro, California as an introduced ornamental and as a native plant very locally in extreme southwestern Arizona. It does not occur in New Mexico. The tree is generally small and open-growing but may reach a height of 36 feet. It is distinguished from the other two paloverdes by the very long rachis to which the very tiny leaflets are attached. The rachis may become as much as 18 inches long and the leaves appear as tiny scales, borne in pairs. There is a pair of short spines at the base of each leaf rachis. The flowers are very similar to those of other paloverdes except as the flower fades the banner becomes orange or red. The wood of this species is very similar to the other paloverdes, but it is lighter yellow in color.

In generaly, the paloverdes, associated with saguaro cactus, mesquite, catclaw, and ironwood, dominate the landscape over a

Yellow paloverde

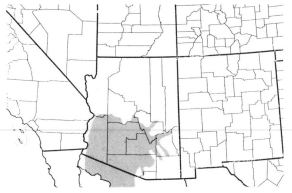

Yellow paloverde

Blue paloverde

vast area of southern Arizona and south-eastern California. They do provide some browsing for domestic stock and deer. The seeds are eaten by quail and white-winged doves and may be very valuable to the latter. They furnish scant shade as the leaves, small as they are, fall off during dry spells. The wood may be used locally for firewood.

It is of interest that the leafless stems and green trunks bear chlorophyll and are thus able to carry on manufacture of food for the plant in the absence of leaves.

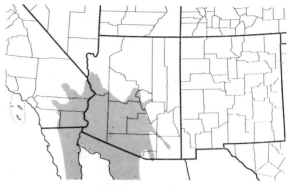

Blue paloverde

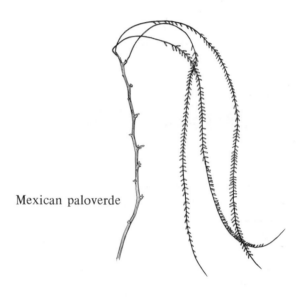

Mexican paloverde

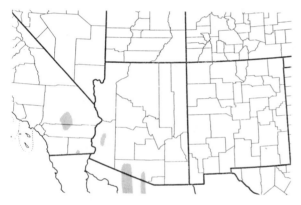

Mexican paloverde

Mexican paloverde

LEGUME FAMILY
(Leguminosae)

Catclaw mimosa or wait-a-minute— *Mimosa biuncifera*
"Una de gato"
Velvetpod mimosa—*Mimosa dysocarpa*
"Gatuno"
Fragrant mimosa—*Mimosa borealis*
Lindheimer mimosa—*Mimosa lindheimeri*
Warnock mimosa—*Mimosa warnockii*
Graham mimosa—*Mimosa grahamii*

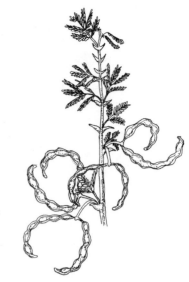

Catclaw mimosa

Mimosa is derived from the word *mimos*, to mimic, and refers to the rapid, animal-like movements of the leaves. *Biuncifera* refers to the stout, paired thorns; *dysocarpa* means hard seed; *borealis* refers to the plant's northern distribution; and names of the last three species listed all honor men.

Catclaw mimosa or wait-a-minute bush occurs in the Lower Sonoran Zone in New Mexico and southeastern Arizona, thence northwest through central Arizona to Kingman. Catclaw mimosa is usually a shrub to about 6 feet in height but may become as tall as 10 feet and 2 inches in diameter in favorable places. It has a pair of recurved spines at the nodes of the twigs where the twice-compound leaves are also attached. The leaves are up to nearly 2 inches long; 4 to 7 pairs of primary leaflets, each with up to 12 pairs of tiny leaflets on the secondary rachis. The pale pink to whitish flowers occur in globose, crowded heads. The seed pods are about 1½ inches long, often curved, and with margins of the pod prickly or smooth. The sapwood is light yellowish white and the heart is deep reddish brown, very similar to mescat acacia.

Velvetpod mimosa occurs in the Chiricahua Mountains of southeastern Arizona and westward through Cochise, Santa Cruz, and Pima Counties to the Boboquivara Mountains and in southwestern New Mexico. It grows as a shrub to about 6 feet in height. The leaves are up to 2 inches long, bicompound with 5 to 12 pairs of primary leaflets and each with 6 to 16 pairs of tiny leaflets. The pink to lavender flowers occur in crowded spikes about 1 inch long and ½ inch in diameter. The short spikes are irregularly spaced along the stem.

Fragrant mimosa occurs as a shrub to 6 feet in height in New Mexico and eastward in Oklahoma and Texas. The leaves are small, bicompound, with only 2 secondary pinnae, each with 3 to 8 pairs of small leaflets. The showy pink flowers are crowded into round heads on slender stalks attached to the twigs

Catclaw mimosa

Catclaw mimosa

Velvetpod mimosa

at the leaf axils. The pods are 1 to 2 inches long with several seeds per pod.

Lindheimer mimosa is sometimes considered as a variety of catclaw mimosa but has more glabrous flowers and leaves and fewer secondary leaflets. The range is similar to catclaw mimosa and the two may intergrade. The flowers occur in round pink heads.

Warnock mimosa is a low-growing shrub forming a mound about 3 feet high. The small white flowers occur in round heads on short stalks. The pods are small, somewhat prickly on the margins, and not constricted between the seeds.

Graham mimosa occurs in southeastern Arizona and southwestern New Mexico as a low bush only about 1½ feet in height. The leaves are up to 4 inches long, bi-pinnately compound with up to 8 pairs of primary divisions, each with 8 to 15 pairs of small leaflets. Round flower heads occur on short stalks. The pods are small and prickly. The twigs are reddish brown with short, curved, or straight spines, generally at the axils of the leaves.

The mimosas are not important range plants but may be utilized as a reserve food supply. Deer browse them somewhat and quail and rodents utilize the seeds. The plants furnish shade and cover and serve to protect the soil.

LEGUME FAMILY
(Leguminosae)

Honey mesquite—*Prosopis juliflora* var.
    glandulosa
Western honey mesquite—*P. juliflora* var.
    torreyana
Velvet mesquite—*P. juliflora* var. *velutina*
Screwbean or "tornillo"—*P. pubescens*
"Mezquite" is the Spanish name for all but the last named.

Prosopis is an old Greek word for burdock but the application is obscure. *Juliflora* is derived from *julus* or catkin-like flower spike. *Glandulosa* is for the glandular anther

Fragrant mimosa

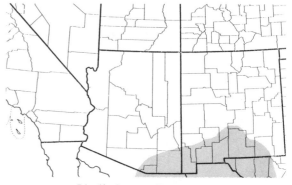

Lindheimer mimosa
and
Warnock mimosa

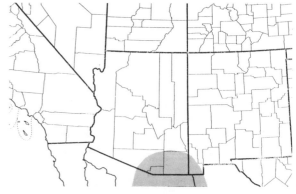

Graham mimosa
(4,000 to 6,000)

Western honey mesquite

connections of the flowers; *torreyana* honors John Torrey, botanist; *velutina* refers to the velvety leaves; and *pubescens* to downy soft hairs.

Generally in non-technical writing, the three varieties of mesquite are lumped together without specifying a variety name. It is difficult to separate them on the basis of clear-cut botanical differences. In our area, honey mesquite occurs in west Texas and west into eastern New Mexico. It is hard to say exactly where honey mesquite stops and western honey mesquite begins, but the range of mountains east of the Rio Grande appears to separate the two, although Benson and Darrow list the former as far west as Silver City. Western honey mesquite covers large areas of southwestern New Mexico. Velvet mesquite then becomes most common across Arizona and western honey mesquite again assumes dominance in southeastern California. Velvet mesquite occurs in southwestern New Mexico, as far east as Las Cruces. Screwbean is scattered throughout the west from the Rio Grande in New Mexico and Texas, west to near San Bernardino, California, and north into southern Nevada and southwestern Utah. It appears to be more often found along stream courses and water holes than are the mesquites.

In honey mesquite the larger secondary leaflets are 1 to 2 or 2½ inches long, 9 to 11 times as long as broad, spaced commonly 3/8 to 3/4 inch apart, and the seeds are ellipsoidal, about twice as long as broad. In eastern New Mexico it is characteristically a shrub but becomes treelike in Texas. It frequently grows on sandy soil, and if the grass is grazed heavily, sand drifts into the mesquite plants producing a very rough, dunelike terrain. Much of southern New Mexico is so affected. The flowers of the mesquites are borne in long, narrow, cylindrical, light yellow heads. The wood of honey mesquite has light yellow sapwood, medium brown heartwood, and is hard and heavy.

Western honey mesquite, to continue from Benson and Darrow, has smaller secondary leaflets 3/5 to 7/8 inch long, 7 to 9 times as long as broad, spaced usually ¼ inch apart; seeds obovate, 1½ times as long as broad. It is doubtful if the woods of honey and western honey mesquite can be distinguished.

Velvet mesquite has short, dense hairs covering practically the entire plant, including the pods; leaflets 3½ to 4 times as long as broad; pods with beaks 1/12 to ¼ or

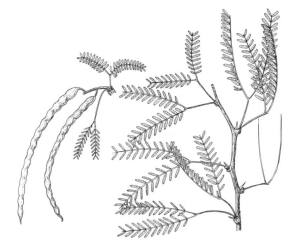

Western honey mesquite

Velvet mesquite (left)
Western honey mesquite (right)

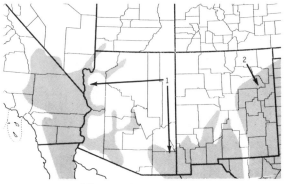

1. Western honey mesquite
2. Honey mesquite

rarely ½ inch long; primary leaflets in 2 pairs in perhaps half the leaves. It has been my observation that both the honey mesquites show prominently enlarged nodes at the leaf axils where the spines are attached. Velvet mesquite lacks these enlarged nodes. Pictures in botanical journals show this, but it is not mentioned as a fixed character. The wood of velvet mesquite, when first cut, is a very pronounced lavender color and cures much brighter red than the brown wood of the honey mesquites. Mesquite pods are cylindrical, about ¼ inch in diameter, and up to 6 inches long, straw-colored, and often clustered.

Screwbeans are readily recognized when in fruit by the strikingly and tightly twisted seed pods, in contrast to the straight pods of the mesquites. The leaves of screwbean are similar to western honey mesquite. The wood is hard and heavy with beautiful striped grain produced by the alternation of the light brown spring wood and the dark brown summer wood in the heartwood. The thin sapwood is straw-colored.

The mesquites are troubled by a natural enemy, an insect that girdles the bark of smaller branchlets, causing the ends to die. This tends to keep the plants low and shrub-like. Another factor in keeping them low in growth form is frost. In years when the winters are severe, the plants are killed to the ground in the northern extensions of their range. They are quick to sprout again from the roots the following spring. Fourwing saltbush grows in association with mesquite over much of its range, and it is a common sight to see a tall saltbush growing up in the center of a clump of mesquite. Saltbush is very palatable to grazing animals, and in the center of the mesquite clump it is protected until it grows large enough to withstand the grazing it gets in such a situation.

The mesquite clumps furnish excellent cover for all types of birds and small mammals of the desert. In fact, an acre of mesquite range has been found to produce more pounds of rodents than of beef! The seeds are eaten by quail and doves. Along with paloverde in Arizona, mesquites are very valuable to white-winged doves. Mesquite is browsed by deer but apparently not as a preferred food.

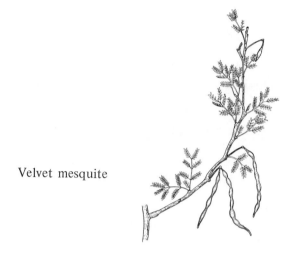

Velvet mesquite

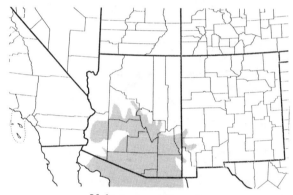

Velvet mesquite

Screwbean

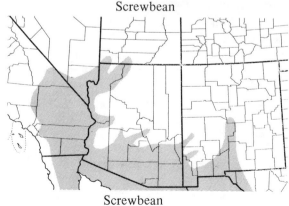

Screwbean

78

LEGUME FAMILY
(*Leguminosae*)

The following gives common name (1), distribution (2), characteristics (3), and uses (4) of leguminous plants.

INDIGOBUSH. (2) Streambanks, N.M. and eastward. (3) Variable in size, generally small shrub, compound leaves to 10" long, 10-pair leaflets. Long terminal, reddish-purple flower spike. (4) Food or cover use limited. Wood too small to be useful.

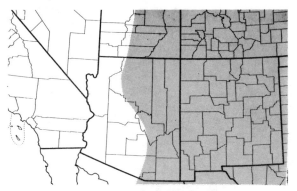

Indigobush (Amphora fruticosa)

FALSE MESQUITE ("Cabello de Angel"). (2) Lower Sonoran Zone, N.M. to Calif. (3) Low dense shrub to 3'. Small leaves twice compound, leaflets tiny. Flowers loose globose heads, white to purple. (4) Valuable browse plant for game and stock. Seeds taken by quail. Wood too small to be useful.

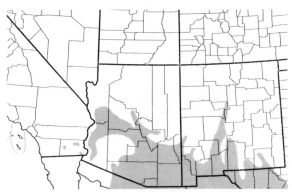

False mesquite (Calliandra eriophylla)

SENNA. (2) SW N.M., SE Ariz. to 5,000 ft. (3) Shrub to 9'. Alternate, compound leaves with few, small leaflets. Flowers yellow in many-flowered axillary or terminal heads. (4) Cover. Wood too small.

1. Senna (Cassia wislizeni)
2. Senna (Cassia roemeriana)

WESTERN REDBUD . (2) Grand Canyon to Rainbow Bridge. S Utah, S Nev., Calif. (3) Shrub to small tree. Simple, rounded leaves heartshaped. Purplish flowers pealike in clusters on old wood. (4) Cover. Too scarce to be of much value. Wood too small and

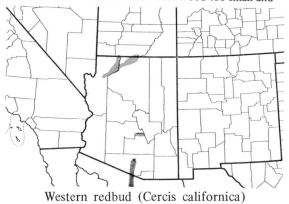

Western redbud (Cercis californica)

BUNDLE FLOWER. (2) SE Ariz., Chiricahua N.M. (3) Small halfshrub; compound leaves, twisted pod, small green or whitish flowers in terminal spikes. (4) Uses not known; wood too small.

Bundle flower (Desmanthus cooleyi)

CORALBEAN, SOUTHWESTERN ("Colorin," "Coralina"). (2) SW N.M., SE Ariz. (3) Shrub or small tree. Alternate deciduous leaves with 3 paddle-like leaflets. Red flowers in showy terminal spikes. Seeds scarlet. (4) Seeds very poisonous. Too scarce to be of use. Wood soft and corky.

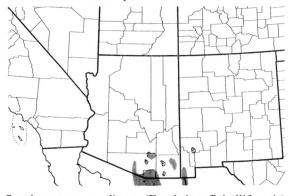

Southwestern coralbean (Erythrina flabelliformis)
and
Kidneywood (Eysenhardtia polystachya) (solid)

KIDNEYWOOD. ("Palo dulce"). (2) SW New Mexico, SE Ariz. (3)Shrub or possibly small tree. Many stems. Long, compound leaves with up to 20 pair leaflets. Small white flowers in axillary spikes. (4) Supposed to have medical value for kidney, bladder infections. Valuable deer browse. Sapwood yellow, heart light reddish brown, hard, heavy and dense.

INDIGO. (2) SE Ariz., Chiricahua, N.M. (3) Shrubs to 4 ft., compound leaves. Many leaflets, flowers in axillary spikes, white or pink, pods small, ball-like, 1-seeded. (4) Browsed, used in erosion control. Wood use not known.

Golden-ball lead tree

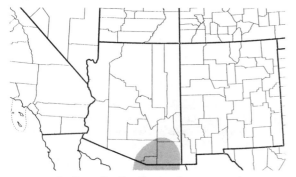

Indigo (Indigofera sphaerocarpa)

Golden-ball lead tree (Leucaena retusa)

RATANY, RANGE. (2) Desert grassland Lower Sonoran Zone N.M., Ariz., SW Utah, So. Nev., west. (3)Small, intricately branched shrub to 2'. Simple, gray alternate leaves very small. Showy purplish flowers axillary. Small globose seed pods. (4) Important forage, w. ranges. Burrlike seed pods readily dist. Wood too small.

IRONWOOD, TESOTA ("Palo de Hierro" or "Tesota"). (2) Lower desert of Ariz. and SE Calif. (3)Spiny tree to 30', short trunk. Evergreen leaves numerous and gray-green. Pealike, purplish flowers in clusters. 2¼" pod, few seeds. (4) Seeds edible when roasted. Plant valuable for food, cover,erosion control. One of the hardest, heaviest woods. Dark brown.

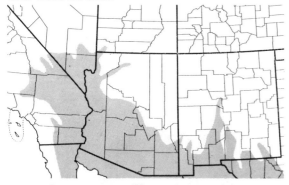

Range ratany (Krameria parvifolia)

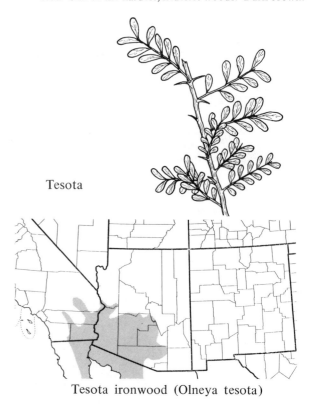

Tesota

GOLDEN-BALL LEAD TREE. (2) Guadalupe Mts., SE N.M. and south. (3) Shrub or small tree to 25'. Leaves bipinnate with 3 to 4 prs. leaflets. Yellow, globose glower heads borne axillary. Long, slender seed pods. (4) Readily browsed by cattle. Too scarce in our area to be of value. Brown wood, hard and heavy.

Tesota ironwood (Olneya tesota)

DUNEBROOM. (2) Sandy hills No. N.M., Ariz.
(3) Low shrub, broomlike branches. Slender twigs,
tiny leaves, terminal flowers yellowish green. Tiny
1-seeded pods. (4) Cover, erosion control. Wood too
small.

Dunebroom

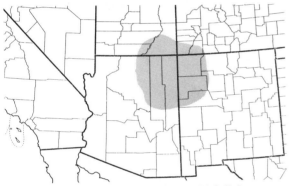

Dunebroom (Parryella filifolia)

NEW MEXICO LOCUST ("Una de gato"). (2)Mts.,
Transition and mixed conifer, N.M., Ariz., No. and
west to Calif. (3) Spiny shrub or small, slender tree
to 25'. Leaves compound, 15 to 21 leaflets. Large,
showy, purplish flowers in terminal clusters, pea-
like. Shrub or very small tree. Not spiny. (4) Used
lightly by game or not at all in many areas. Good
cover. Wood very hard with greenish color.

New Mexico locust

New Mexico locust

New Mexico locust (Robinia neomexicana)

MESCALBEAN ("Frijolillo"). (2) SE N.M. and
Texas. (3) Leaves dark shiny green, evergreen, 7 to
13 per stem. Pealike purplish flowers. Seed pods
1½ to 4" long. Thick scarlet beans. (4) Seeds poisonous. One will kill a person. Too scarce to be of
value. Wood hard, heavy, orange with red streaks.

Mescalbean

81

Mescalbean

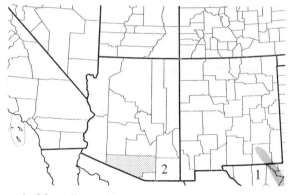

1. Mescalbean (Sophora secundiflora)
2. Littleleaf lysiloma (Lysiloma microphylla)
   Pima county, Arizona

LILY FAMILY
(Liliaceae)

Soaptree yucca—*Yucca elata*
"Palmilla"
Torrey yucca—*Yucca torreyi*
"Palma criolla"
Schott's yucca—*Yucca schottii*
Joshua tree—*Yucca brevifolia*

Yucca is a native Haitian word mis-applied to our plant. Several species occur in our area as shrubs only and never become treelike. Those reported from parks and monuments of our area include: *Y. baccata*, the Datil yucca of the Southwest; *Y. navajoa* or Navajo yucca; *Y. angustissima*, narrowleaf yucca of the northeast; *Y. standleyi*, Standley yucca; *Y. intermedia*, intermediate yucca; *Y. harrimaniae*, Harriman yucca; *Y. glauca*, small soapweed yucca, for which the name *Y. angustifolia* is a synonym; *Y. arizonica, Y. whippeli* and *Y. baileyi*. Of the treelike yuccas we have four species: Soaptree, Torrey, Schott's, and Joshua tree.

LITTLELEAF LYSILOMA ("Quiebracha" or "Tepe guaje"). (2) Rincon Mts., Pima Co., Ariz. (3) Leaves large, 4-9 pairs primary leaflets. About 30 pairs secondary leaflets. Flowers globular, white, 3/4" dia. Pod oblong, large, flat, smooth with many seeds. (4) Too scarce to be of value. Wood hard, dark brown, brittle.

Soaptree yucca

Soaptree yucca gets the specific name from its tall, slender growth form. This is the most widespread of the treelike yuccas. It occurs from south of Albuquerque on the Rio Grande, south to the southern border and west across the State. In Arizona it occurs in the southern and central parts to the Salt River and west to Salome. It also extends into northern Mexico. This most slender of the treelike yuccas is distinguished by its tall flower stalk, tallest of the yuccas. This yucca may be branched. The fruits are short and contain paper-thin seeds. The plant is the New Mexico State Flower.

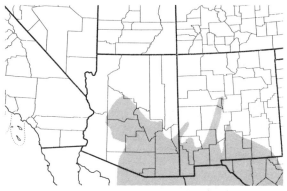

Soaptree yucca

Schott's yucca was named for Arthur C. V. Schott, a German-American naturalist who collected for the U.S.-Mexican Border Survey in the 1850's. It may occur in extreme southwest New Mexico and does occur in the Chiricahua Mountains of Arizona and west to the Santa Catalina Mountains in Pima and Pinal Counties.

Schott's yucca has a short flower stalk and the fruits appear to be clustered in the leaves at the top of the plant. This yucca is often branched. The leaves are quite long and heavy but without threads along the edges. The banana-like fruits are about 4 inches long and half as broad.

Torrey yucca

Torrey yucca has a very limited range in south-central New Mexico. I found it on the west slope of the Sacramento Mountains east of Alamogordo and near Carlsbad, New Mexico. It will be recognized immediately by the long, white threads growing along edges of the bayonet-like, thick, heavy leaves and by short flower stalk. This yucca has a single, unbranched trunk.

Joshua tree, in far western Arizona and California, will be recognized immediately by its height and multiple branching. It also has a short flower stalk and large fruits. This is the only one of the yuccas having a dense enough trunk to be considered woodlike. Even so, I found it necessary to glue my sample to a sheet of plywood to keep it from falling apart. The other yuccas have a soft, fibrous, pulpy trunk that is not woodlike.

Just before the fruits of the shorter yuccas mature, they are avidly eaten by livestock. These yuccas furnish nesting sites for birds of the desert and escape cover for birds and small mammals. Yucca flowers are eaten by deer when they can reach them. Even the sharp spines of the yucca leaves have been found in the stomachs of deer, Barbary sheep, and antelope and will, no doubt, be found in stomachs of oryx released in southwestern

Torrey yucca

deserts. Cattle eat the bases of Datil yuccas and javelinas tear plants apart to get at the tender leaf bases. Thus, inhospitable as they appear, yuccas still serve a useful purpose for wildlife.

Yuccas resemble agaves superficially but may be distinguished by the presence of tree-like trunks in several species, lack of hard, sharp terminal and side spines on leaves, presence of lily-like flowers in season and later, banana-like fruits. Agaves send up one tall, slender flower stalk and die, whereas yuccas live on to bloom again and again.

Schott's yucca

Schott's yucca

Joshua tree

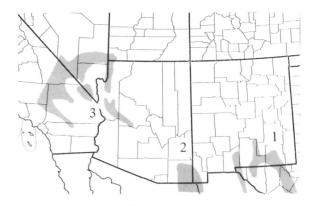

1. Torrey yucca
2. Schott's yucca
3. Joshua tree

MAPLE FAMILY
(Aceraceae)

Rocky Mountain maple
Acer glabrum
Bigtooth maple
Acer grandidentatum
Boxelder
Acer negundo
'Acecinele"

Acer is the Latin word for the genus and means hard or sharp. Of the specific names, *glabrum* means smooth, *grandidentatum* means bigtooth, and *negundo* is a Malay name for a tree with similar leaves.

Rocky Mountain maple occurs in the high mountains throughout the western two-thirds and northeastern New Mexico, and in Arizona from the southeast corner north and west to the Grand Canyon. Its range extends on north to Canada. In our area it occurs along streams in the ponderosa and mixed conifer zones from about 7,000 feet to 9,000 feet or more. It generally occurs as a many-stemmed shrub, but occasionally makes a small tree. The leaves are 3-lobed with the edges sharply toothed. The small inconspicuous flowers occur in winged pairs called samaras. The bark is smooth and thin. The wood is moderately hard, dense, and close-grained. The color varies from light brown, streaked with dark grey to almost black. This gives it an interesting grain pattern. The wood does not grow large enough for commercial purposes, but it cures easily without serious checking. It can be used for turning small items from a section of the trunk. The seeds are taken by squirrels and possibly other wildlife. Some deer use has been recorded. Its chief use is as a component of the cover.

Bigtooth maple occurs in canyons and on moist soil in the mountains of central and southern New Mexico, in most of the high mountains of Arizona except northeastern and and southwestern parts, and north to Montana and Idaho. It occurs in the ponderosa pine zone. This maple develops into a good-sized tree in favorable sites, 50 or more feet tall and 1 foot or more in diameter. The leaves are typically 3-lobed, with broad, blunt lobes not finely toothed. The flowers and seeds are similar to Rocky Mountain maples. The bark is gray to light brown, and the wood is hard, heavy, and light straw-colored. Although the trees are large enough to be of

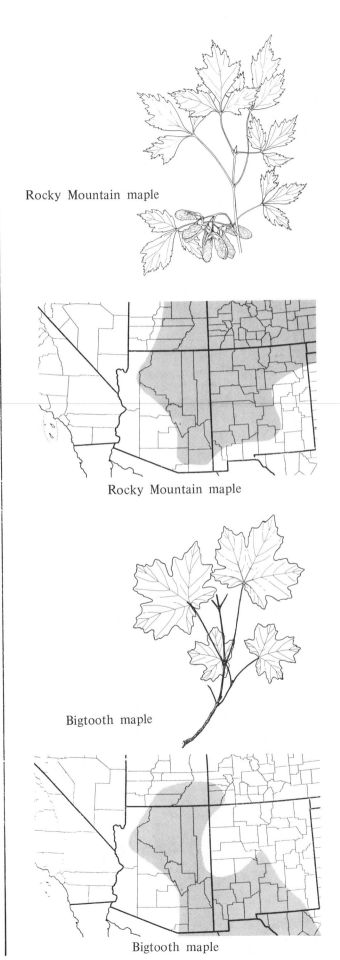

Rocky Mountain maple

Rocky Mountain maple

Bigtooth maple

Bigtooth maple

commercial value, there are not enough of them to be worth harvesting. Their value to wildlife is similar to that of Rocky Mountain maple, but more limited because of the small number of trees.

Boxelder is widely distributed in the lower mountains and foothills throughout our area and north to Canada. It has also been used in the towns and settlements as an ornamental. It is considered objectionable because it attracts boxelder beetles and exudes sticky droplets from the foliage. It develops into a medium-sized tree, often with several stems to a clump. It has a wide crown and very rough rough, knobby, burled trunks. The paired leaves vary from other maples in that they are 3- to 5-lobed with the terminal lobe stalked. The flowers and seeds are similar to the other maples.

The wood is relatively soft, nearly white with areas of pink in larger logs, and tends to discolor quickly in the cut log. In areas where magpies occur, this is the preferred nesting tree. Any wildlife value that it may have would be as nesting cover for birds and, perhaps, for browse to a limited degree. Barbary sheep have been known to browse it at times. It serves as resting cover.

Bigtooth maple (leaf detail)

Bigtooth maple (bark detail)

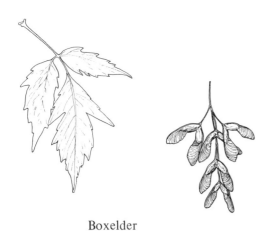

Boxelder

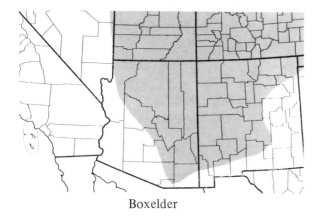

Boxelder

MULBERRY FAMILY
(Moraceae)

Texas mulberry or Littleleaf mulberry—
    Morus microphylla
"Mora, moral"

    Morus is the classical name for the genus, and *microphylla* literally means small-leafed. This tree is rather hard to find, as it grows in the same niche as netleaf hackberry and resembles it enough to be confusing. It occurs in southern New Mexico and southeastern Arizona. It is thinly scattered and is generally associated with limestone hills. I found a nice specimen in the Chiricahua Mountains, one in the Organ Mountains, and have been told that it is fairly abundant in the Silver City area in New Mexico.

    The wood is hard and heavy, dark orange to brown in color with a thin, straw-colored sapwood. The berries are red to black in color and smaller than the domestic varieties. The trees are small, about 20 feet tall and a few to several inches in diameter. The leaves may have the typical lobed shape of the domestic mulberries, but many of the leaves fail to develop lobes. They are small, about two inches long, and have serrated edges.

    The berries are valuable for wildlife. It is said that some Indians have cultivated mulberry trees for their berries.

Texas mulberry

Texas mulberry

Texas mulberry

NIGHTSHADE FAMILY
(Solanaceae)

Pale wolfberry—*Lycium pallidum*
Anderson wolfberry—*L. andersonii*
Berlandier wolfberry—*L. berlandieri*
"Cilindrillo"
Fremont lycium—*L. fremontii*
Torrey lycium—*L. torreyi*
"Garambullo"
Cooper lycium—*L. cooperi*
Parish lycium—*L. parishii*
Macrodon lycium—*L. macrodon*
Lycium—*L. exsertum*

All of the above lyciums or wolfberries are reported from our area, but only the first three are very common or widespread. *Lycium* is named for the country of Lycia. *Pallidum* means pale, referring to the leaves and flowers. The next six specific names honor various men.

The first three species named above have widespread occurrence from western Texas, through New Mexico, Arizona, and south into Mexico. The others are of more local occurrence, largely in western Arizona and on into southern California. Torrey lycium is reported to grow in New Mexico. Pale wolfberry extends the farthest north, into southwest Colorado and southern Utah. It also occurs at the highest elevations. Most of the other ones are desert plants.

Wolfberries may occur as single plants or as thickets. They are normally 3 to 6 feet high and spiny. The small clustered leaves and tubular flowers, greenish-yellow in color, serve as the best identifying characteristics. The red fruit, with 20 to 50 seeds in a berry, gives the plant some value in naturalistic plantings. Birds eat the berries and livestock browse the bushes if more desirable feed is scarce. Use by big game is not important. Anderson wolfberry is often larger -growing than pale wolfberry. Wolfberries are frequently found around old Indian ruins, probably indicating that the berries were gathered and used.

Pale wolfberry

Pale wolfberry is found throughout the area, except in the high mountains and in the southwestern Arizona desert.

Pale wolfberry

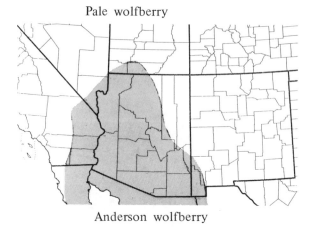

Anderson wolfberry

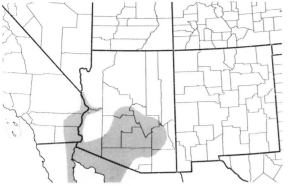

Fremont lycium

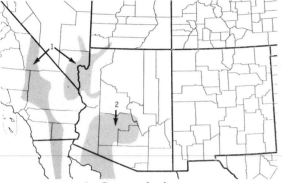

1. Cooper lycium
2. Macrodon lycium

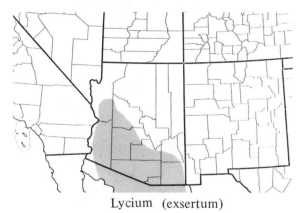

Lycium (exsertum)

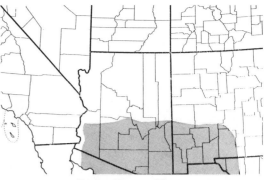

Berlandier wolfberry

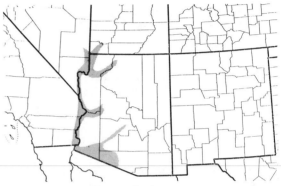

Torrey lycium

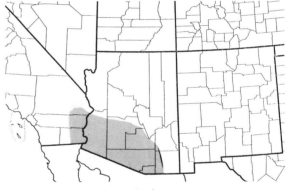

Parish lycium

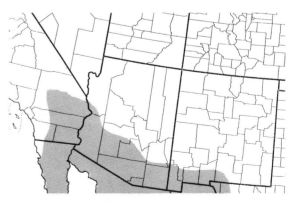

Tree tobacco

NIGHTSHADE FAMILY
(Solanaceae)

Tree tobacco— *Nicotiana glauca*
"Corneton," "Virgino"

The genus name honors Jean Nicot, a French diplomat, and *glauca* refers to the whitish bloom covering the leaves and stems.

This is another introduced plant that has escaped from cultivation and now occurs in the southern part of our area. It grows as a tall shrub. The simple, alternate leaves are nearly evergreen, up to 1 foot long and 3 inches wide. The yellowish green, tubular flowers occur in terminal panicles. The oblong seed capsules open at the apex. The plant contains an alkaloid that is said to be poisonous if swallowed.

89

OCOTILLO FAMILY
(Fouquieriaceae)

Ocotillo—*Fouquieria splendens*
"Ocotillo" or "Albarda"

Ocotillo

The generic name honors P. E. Fouquier of France. It is called *splendens* because of the spectacular flowers. This is one of our most distinctive shrubs. It consists of a clump of tall, straight sticks arising from a crown and slanting outward like an inverted cone. During dry spells the sticks look dead. Soon after a good rain they leaf out with small bright green leaves along the length of the stick, making it look about twice the thickness it did before. In season the tops of the stems are crowned by a spike of very bright red flowers, tubular in shape and each about 1 inch long. The leaves fall off when the weather turns dry, but the red flowers remain even after the leaves fall. The plant ranges across dry rocky hillsides from west Texas across southern New Mexico and Arizona to California.

The ocotillo stems become as much as 20 feet tall and up to 3 inches in diameter in good sites. The wood is nearly white, soft, and moderately heavy when green. The bark is dark gray, rough, and scaly. On large stems, the bark breaks and shows an under-layer of thin, scaly, light yellow bark.

In spite of the protection given this plant by its very thorny nature, deer browse it freely and ibex are reported to literally tear the plant apart in browsing it.

Ocotillo

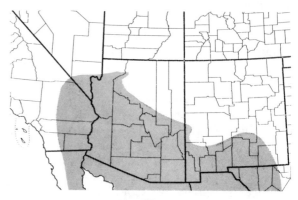

Ocotillo

OLEASTER FAMILY
(Elaeagnaceae)

Russian olive—*Elaeagnus angustifolia*

Russian olive

The generic name is made up of *Elae*, from the Greek for olive, and *agn*, from Greek for pure or innocent. The specific name means means narrow-leaved. Thus, it becomes the pure olive with narrow leaves. This tree grows along watercourses in the Southwest from about 7,000 feet elevation down throughout the length of the stream courses in the area. The tree is small and generally many-branched with narrow silvery leaves, strong-smelling flowers, and seeds covered with silvery scales, produced abundantly. The trees have numerous long, sharp thorns. The seeds are readily eaten by many species of birds, including passerine birds, game birds, and waterfowl, particularly if the locality is flooded in winter. The foliage is browsed by deer and livestock, and the almost impenetrable thickets are good game cover. The wood is moderately heavy, hard, and dense with light-brown spring wood and dark-brown summer wood, which gives a striking banded appearance. The wood is not considered to be of commercial importance.

Russian olive is another of the introduced trees that has become naturalized. Introduced from Russia as a shade and windbreak tree, it is generally considered to have been a good introduction. It has been planted widely throughout our area and has spread along stream courses. No distribution map is needed.

Russian olive

OLEASTER FAMILY
(Eleagnaceae)

Silver buffaloberry—*Shepherdia argentea*
Russet buffaloberry—*S. canadensis*
Round-leaf buffaloberry—*S. rotundifolia*

    Shepherdia honors John Shepherd; *argentea* refers to the silvery scales on the leaves; *canadensis* refers to northern distribution; *rotundifolia* means round leaf.

    Silver buffaloberry is not listed by some authors as a tree in our area; however, a clump with treelike stems about 6 inches in diameter and 20 feet tall occurs in northern New Mexico near the Ghost Ranch in Rio Arriba County. The bright, silvery leaves, about ½ inch wide and 2 inches long, make this shrub stand out among the oaks and other trees with which it is associated. The twigs are spiny and the berries are borne along the stems below the leaves. Deer are known to have used this plant in the Guadalupe Mountains. The sapwood is very light straw color, while the heartwood is light and dark brown streaked in a bold grain pattern. The wood is light, soft, and weak. The range of this plant extends through the plains and canyons in the pinon-juniper zone in New Mexico, Utah, Colorado, and eastward.

    Russet buffaloberry is a shrub, generally about 4 to 6 feet tall in our area, the clumps made up of slender stems. The leaves have rust-colored scales and the younger twigs are covered with them, also. The leaves are dark green and not as long and slender as in the silver buffaloberry. The berries of both buffaloberries are considered edible but are bitter. They are readily taken by many species of birds, small mammals, and by deer, to some extent. The third species, *S. rotundifolia*, occurs in the Grand Canyon and north into Utah.

Russet buffaloberry

Russet buffaloberry

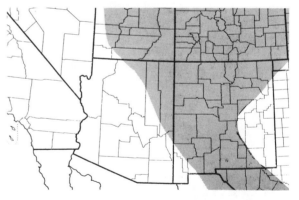

Silver buffaloberry and Russet buffaloberry (broad range essentially the same for both species, but Silver buffaloberry generally occurs at higher altitudes within the range.)

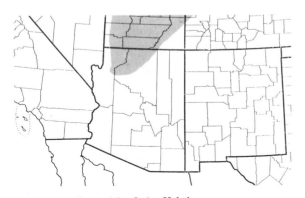

Round-leaf buffaloberry

PALM FAMILY
(Palmae)

California fan palm or washingtonia—
    Washingtonia filifera
"Palma de Castilla"

    The genus was dedicated to President George Washington. *Filifera* means thread-bearing and refers to the threadlike fibers along leaf edges.

    The only palm native to our area, the California fan palm, occurs in Palm Canyon on the west side of the Kofa Mountains south of Quartsite, Arizona. The locality may be reached by a road that branches off the main highway about 19 miles south of Quartsite. It also occurs in various places named Palm Canyons, Palm Springs, etc., in California around the northern and western portions of the Salton Sea basin and on the margin of the Mohave Desert. It has also been propagated and used extensively for landscape plantings in Arizona and California.

    This palm, in natural condition, appears short and stocky. It normally attains a height of 20 to 80 feet. The old leaves die and fold downward around the trunk so that the trunk appears heavily skirted. In landscape work these old leaves are normally cut off, leaving a rough appearance to the trunk unless the leaf-stalk bases are in turn trimmed; then the trunk has a smooth, brown appearance.

    The leaves are palmately divided and fan-shaped. A palmate leaf is divided around the outer edge, but the divisions are united farther down as are the fingers and palm of a human hand. The edges of these divisions are lightly fringed with brownish strings. The flowers occur in several long, loose, drooping panicles. The small seeds are enclosed in a nearly black shell. The solitary seed is tan or brown. These were used by Indians for food. This may account for the occurrence of the palms in many scattered groves.

California fan palm

California fan palm

93

PINE FAMILY
(Pinaceae)

White fir—*Abies concolor*

White fir is one of the three true firs which occur in the Southwest. *Abies* is the Latin name for the genus; *concolor* means having uniform color. White fir is seldom a major component of the forest stand, as it occurs scattered throughout the forest. White fir grows to a height of 100 feet or more and 3 feet in diameter, or more. It is the largest true fir of the region. White fir occurs at lower altitudes in the forest than the other firs. It is found in the upper part of the ponderosa pine zone and on into the mixed conifer zone above.

The needles of white fir are the longest of the firs and may become 3 inches long. They are broad, flat, and silver-blue in color, giving rise to the common name. The inconspicuous flowers are borne in the spring and are dark rose red. The cones may become as much as 5 inches long. These grow upright on the higher limbs and appear to be perched like candles on the tops of the branchlets upon which they are growing. The cones of all firs disintegrate while still attached to the tree, which explains why whole cones are not seen on the ground. Squirrels often cut whole cones before they fall apart and store them in caches.

The bark of young firs is smooth and generally gray to white, with numerous blisters containing balsam, a very sticky substance. As the trees mature, the bark of white fir tends to break up into elongated plates with deep furrows between the ridges.

The true firs are not highly valuable to wildlife, partly because the trees are scattered in the forest, partly because the forage is of relatively poor quality. However, the seeds are readily eaten by squirrels, grouse, and several species of forest-loving birds, and the young growth is browsed by deer and mountain sheep at times. Otherwise, their chief value is as another component of the cover required by all wildlife.

The wood of white fir is taken along with spruce and other trees with which it grows. About 30 million board feet of fir are harvested per year in the Southwest. This includes all three species. The wood of white fir is white with very light brown to slightly purplish streaks, not strong, but suitable for sheathing and other modern construction needs where strength is not important.

White fir

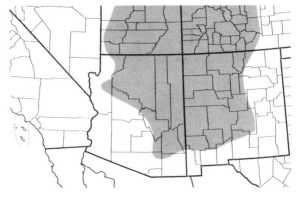

White fir

94

PINE FAMILY
(Pinaceae)

Corkbark fir—*Abies lasiocarpa* var. *arizonica*

Corkbark fir is the second most plentiful fir in the Southwest. It grows higher in the mountains than white fir, where it is often co-dominant with Engelmann spruce. *Lasiocarpa* means having wooly fruit, and refers to the downy covering of the cones. The variety is the Latinized version of the name of the State where it was found. Many writers combine corkbark fir with the species *Abies lasiocarpa* without giving recognition to the variety. The variety tends to be a larger tree, grows farther down the mountain below timberline, is not so sharply pointed in tree shape, and has bark that is definitely corky and white. It is possible that all or very nearly all of this fir growing in New Mexico and Arizona is of the variety and should be called corkbark fir. There is probably a line of integration between the two somewhere north of the New Mexico-Colorado boundary line.

The needles of the corkbark fir are dark green, clustered closely on the branchlets, and only about 1 inch long. The inconspicuous flowers, borne in the spring, are dark blue. The cones are 2 to 4 inches long. The cones disintegrate while still attached to the branchlet.

The wood of corkbark is mixed with that of white fir in the trade. It is lighter color, lighter weight and softer, generally. The largest corkbark fir is growing near Ruidoso, New Mexico. It measures 13 feet 9 inches around and 111 feet tall and has a crown spread of 31 feet.

The sex organs of the trees of the Pinaceae will be called flowers, following Little, Vines and others, even though some botanists feel this to be an improper use of the term.

Corkbark fir

Alpine fir

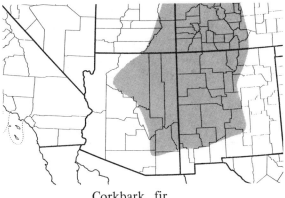

Corkbark fir
and
Alpine fir

95

PINE FAMILY
(Pinaceae)

Alpine or subalpine fir—*Abies lasiocarpa*

Many writers deny recognition to cork-bark fir as a variety *(arizonica)* of this species but group both corkbark and alpine as one tree, *Abies lasiocarpa.* If corkbark fir is a valid variety, however, then I believe that very nearly all of this type of fir in the Southwest should be so classified. I have not seen subalpine fir in New Mexico, but it does occur in Utah as far south as Cedar Breaks National Monument.

Alpine, or subalpine fir as I know it from northern Colorado, occurs just below timberline in a narrow belt. It is very thinly spired, and the bark is not white or corky. Otherwise, the species and the variety are very similar.

This tree is of little value to wildlife except as it helps to produce the cover so badly needed by the animals of this harsh environment. In any forest the presence of several species tends to lessen the danger of total denudation if an insect attack kills one species. In the vulnerable spruce forest this gives the firs a certain value, even though in some cases they are even more vulnerable than the spruce.

PINE FAMILY
(Pinaceae)
(*Cuppressaceae* of Kearney and Peebles)
Common juniper—*Juniperus communis*
All junipers are "Cedro."

Here is an example of the common name and the scientific name being the same except for the Latinization of common to *communis.* This plant has a very wide range through the northern hemisphere, around the world. In the West it extends into New Mexico in the northern mountains, as the southern extension of its range. Here it occurs only as a low shrub, high in the mountains. Elsewhere it reaches the size of a small shrubby tree.

The needles differ from those of other junipers in that the mature needles are awl-shaped and resemble somewhat the seedling foliage of the other jumipers. The sharp-pointed needles occur in whorls about the branches, spreading at right angles to the stem. The short-stalked, bright blue berries ripen in the third season. The heartwood is light brown, soft, and easily worked. The berries

Alpine fir (bark detail)

Common juniper

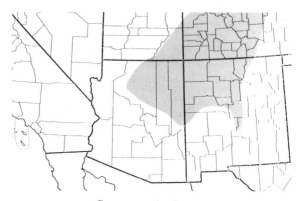

Common juniper

are taken by many species of forest wildlife. They have certain medicinal values and have been used to flavor gin and for a poor coffee substitute.

With such a widespread natural range, this shrub has lent itself well to the propagation of a great variety of forms used in landscape work. These occur under many names, depending on the country where they were originated.

Botanists disagree on the assignment of the family to which junipers belong. Older books use the family *Cuppressaceae*, while newer ones such as Little, Vines, and others place them in the family *Pinaceae*, as I have.

PINE FAMILY
(Pinaceae)

Alligator juniper—*Juniperus deppeana*
"Tascate"

The specific name of this juniper honors Ferdinand Deppe, a German botanist. This species ranges across the southern two-thirds of New Mexico, north to the southern edge of the Jemez Mountains and Mount Taylor and west into southeastern and central Arizona, and south into Mexico. It occurs in about the same niche in its range as do one-seed and Utah junipers in their ranges. It does not lend itself to control as readily as the others because it sprouts from the stump if cut off.

Although this juniper resembles one-seed and Utah juniper very closely, it can be readily distinguished by the "alligator" bark. The bark breaks up into a pattern of small squares, even on small trees. The short, scale-like needles on young trees often have a bluish tinge that makes them easy to mistake at a distance for Rocky Mountain juniper. The largest of all the junipers, alligator juniper, frequently becomes a tree up to 65 feet tall, and it may grow to 5 feet in diameter. The largest known alligator juniper in New Mexico is in the Fort Bayard pasture near Fort Bayard, New Mexico. The American Forestry Association champion is in the Tonto National Forest, Arizona, 29 feet 7 inches in circumference, 57 feet tall, and 57 feet crown.

This juniper bears 2 to 4 seeds per cone in a reddish-brown capsule that is dry and mealy. The cones may be as large as ½ inch in diameter. The wood has some limited commercial importance locally. It is light brown without strong differentiation between the spring and summer wood. It is soft and

Allegator juniper

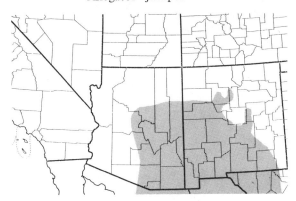

Allegator juniper

carves very nicely, but it is not strong.

Its value to wildlife is similar to that discussed for Rocky Mountain juniper. Where it grows too thickly and covers large areas, it can be thinned out or cleared in a pattern that will improve the habitat for game and the range for domestic stock.

PINE FAMILY
(Pinaceae)

One-seed juniper—*Juniperus monosperma*

Monosperma, the specific name for one-seed juniper, literally means one seed. This juniper ranges from southern Colorado, almost throughout New Mexico, over much of Arizona, parts of Nevada and Utah, and south into Mexico. In Arizona it is largely absent from the northeast and western side. It occurs on drier sites than does Rocky Mountain juniper. In northeast Arizona and in parts of western New Mexico and Utah, it is replaced by Utah juniper.

One-seed juniper has spread through vast areas in the West as a result of heavy grazing by domestic stock. Efforts have been made to control the plant on hundreds of thousands of acres, with varying results. If control is well planned, it can enhance the range for both domestic stock and wild game.

One-seed and Utah juniper are the two most difficult to distinguish in the field. In a general way, one-seed is more likely to be a shrub or small tree, branching from the root collar and lacking a distinct trunk. Utah juniper, on the other hand, is more likely to be treelike with a distinct trunk. Exceptions in both species make positive identification impossible by these characteristics.

Twigs of one-seed juniper tend to be reddish brown. The small yellow flowers are inconspicuous, borne in the spring. The berry is smallest in one-seed juniper, ¼ inch or less in diameter. The berry generally has only one seed, which ripens in the same year that the tree flowers. The cone is copper-colored or rarely blue, thin-fleshed, and moist.

The wood of one-seed juniper may be used locally for posts but generally is of little value. The sapwood is straw-colored and the heart is light brown.

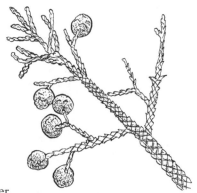

One-seed juniper

One-seed juniper

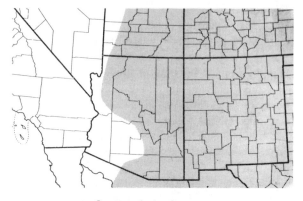

One-seed juniper

98

PINE FAMILY
(Pinaceae)

Utah juniper—*Juniperus osteosperma*

The specific name, *osteosperma*,
literally means bone-seeded. Utah is the center
of its range, with scattered occurrence in
western New Mexico. It is abundant in central
and northeastern Arizona and north into Wyo-
ming. It resembles one-seed juniper in many
of its characteristics, as described under that
species. One good distinguishing feature is
the larger cones that measure from ¼ inch to
over ½ inch in diameter.

Utah juniper is more treelike than one-
seed, has greenish twigs, reddish brown to
bluish berries that are resinous, dry, and
sweet. The wood is generally more valuable
for posts because the tree produces a more
distinct trunk. The wood has straw-colored
sapwood and light brown heart, as does one-
seed. In both these species the twigs are
quite stiff, about 1/16 inch in diameter, with
scalelike leaves, yellowish green in color.

Utah juniper

Utah juniper

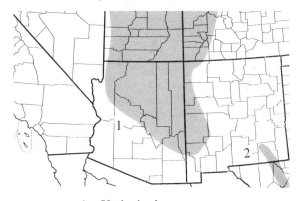

1. Utah juniper
2. Redberry juniper

PINE FAMILY
(Pinaceae)

Redberry juniper—*Juniperus pinchoti*

    The specific name of this tree honors
Gifford Pinchot, one of our early U. S.
foresters. It is more typically a tree of west
Texas but is found in southeast New Mexico
in the Guadalupe Mountains near and in
Carlsbad National Park.
    The cone of redberry is yellow-red to
reddish brown. The small capsules bear a
single, small seed. The greenish twigs become
reddish with age. The growth form is shrubby,
rarely forming a tree in New Mexico but
becomes treelike in Texas. The wood is similar to that of one-seed juniper but lighter
brown in color and is used locally for posts
and fuel. This is another juniper that will
sprout from the stump.

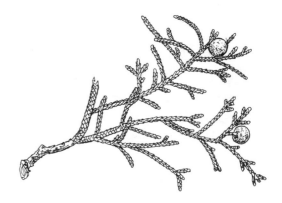

Redberry juniper

PINE FAMILY
(Pinaceae)

Rocky Mountain juniper—*Juniperus
    scopulorum*

    Junipers grow intermingled with pinons
over much of their respective ranges. The
species of juniper varies from one section of
the country to another, just as the species of
pinon varies. At a distance, the pinons and
junipers may be difficult to distinguish. At
closer range, the longer needles of the pines,
growing in bunches, distinguish them from
junipers with their short, scalelike needles.
    The name is derived from the classical
Latin name *Juniperus*, assigned to this genus
of trees. Junipers share the common name
cedar, used throughout the world to name
almost any wood that has the aromatic odor
characteristic of our native junipers. In the
lumber trade, the wood of junipers is nearly
always called cedar. Examples are: eastern
red cedar, characteristic of the eastern states;
Rocky Mountain red cedar, the wood of Rocky
Mountain juniper; and cedar for other junipers. Since the term cedar is used so indis-
criminately, it is better to call our trees
junipers. *Scopulorum* is a Latin word
referring to the habitat of the juniper among
the rocky cliffs and crags.

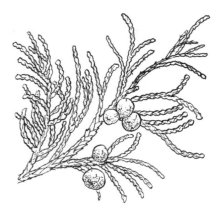

Rocky Mountain juniper

Rocky Mountain juniper

100

The range of Rocky Mountain juniper extends across northwestern two-thirds of New Mexico, the northeastern and north-central part of Arizona, and on north to Canada. This species prefers the moister sites in the foothills and lower mountains.

This juniper, like the other species, grows as a shrub or small tree, occasionally large enough to cut for lumber. Rocky Mountain juniper is often rather conspicuous because of the drooping or weeping form of the silvery leaves. This form is beautiful for landscaping. The flowers are small and inconspicuous and are borne in the spring.

The seed is borne in a cone, but the scales grow together to give it the appearance of a berry. These cones are about ¼ inch in diameter, bright blue from the bloom that covers them. The cone is juicy, generally two-seeded, maturing in the second year. As the tree ages, the bark breaks up into long, thin shreds that hang loosely on the trunk and older branches.

Rocky Mountain juniper, along with the other junipers, is important to wildlife, not only for cover but also for food. The foliage is browsed by deer, desert bighorn sheep, elk, Barbary sheep, and antelope. The seeds are eaten by fox, bear, squirrels, chipmunks, many species of songbirds, deer, wild turkeys, and javelinas.

The wood has long been valued for fuel and fence posts. The heartwood is relatively durable in the ground, but the sapwood rots away readily. Rocky Mountain juniper can be used for cedar chests, specialty products, and other uses similar to those for eastern red cedar when large trees can be found. The growth rings seem poorly cemented together so that the wood may break apart as it is worked. The heartwood is a bright red and the sapwood is straw-colored.

Rocky Mountain juniper

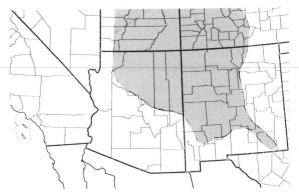

Rocky Mountain juniper

PINE FAMILY
(Pinaceae)

Engelmann spruce—*Picea engelmanni*

The genus name for spruce, *Picea*, is from the ancient Latin *pix* or *picis*, meaning pitch, and the species name honors George Engelmann, a botanist of St. Louis and an authority on conifers. Engelmann spruce grows in dense, pure stands in the Canadian zone, just below timberline on the highest mountain ranges throughout the Southwest.

Englemann spruce is a tall, stately tree. It may reach a height of 165 feet and a diameter of 5 feet in extreme instances. It may also grow as a creeping shrub with the trunk lying along the ground, when it occurs at timberline in the harsh environment of the Hudsonian Zone. The needles of spruce tend to be crowded on the upper side of the branches because the ones from the lower side curve upward to mingle with those on the upper side. Spruce can be distinguished from the other short-needled evergreens by the fact that the needles grow on short pedestals. Thus, when you pick off a needle, this short pedestal is left attached to the twig. This makes the twig appear rough. When a needle is pulled off the true firs and Douglas firs, it leaves only a scar directly on the twig itself, without the pedestal.

The inconspicuous dark purple to scarlet flowers are borne in the spring. Cones are small, from 1 to 2½ inches long. The bark is thin and scaly, cinnamon red to purple brown. When you clasp the end of a twig in the hand, the needles of Engelmann spruce feel soft in contrast to the sharp stiffness of blue spruce needles.

Engelmann spruce is valuable to wildlife, as it covers vast expanses of the higher mountains. The seeds are eaten by many species of birds, and the foliage is browsed by bighorn sheep and deer, sometimes quite heavily. Its chief value to wildlife is in the protection of the high mountain habitat and for furnishing cover for deer, elk, and bighorn sheep, as they move down from the high mountain slopes into the spruce zone with the approach of bad weather. It also forms one of the chief homes for the dusky grouse, which utilizes the buds for food and the trees for protection and roosting sites.

The commercial value of the wood is considerable, since in recent years it has become a desired lumber species. More than 35 million board-feet are cut per year in

Englemann spruce

Englemann spruce

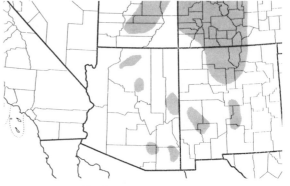

Englemann spruce
(highest mountains)

New Mexico and Arizona. The wood is good for house framing, sheathing, and various other uses. It is nearly white, light in weight and not particularly strong. The surface of the wood tends to case-harden as it cures, and old standing trees in fire-burned areas are exceedingly hard to chop into, but still make good lumber.

The tree is attacked by both bark beetles and spruce bud worm and is subject to windthrow when winds of tornado force blow through the mountains. Thus, many openings valuable to wildlife are created in the forest. Spruce reseeds these openings readily. This sets the stage for succeeding generations of young stands to replace the old mature forest. This tends to maintain a variety of preferred cover for wildlife, and, insofar as the process is a natural one, it is desirable from the game-management standpoint. A similar effect can be obtained by carefully planned cutting that produces similar openings artificially. Care must be taken to keep the areas cut as small as is practical and to make the outline of the cut blend with the topography.

Englemann spruce
(small cone)

PINE FAMILY
(Pinaceae)

Colorado blue spruce—*Picea pungens*

Pungens, the specific name for Colorado blue spruce, means sharp-pointed, which refers to the sharpness of the needles. Clasp a twig in the hand and the point will be made made at once, thus emphasizing the difference between blue spruce and Engelmann spruce.

Colorado blue spruce grows at a lower elevation than Engelmann spruce. It is found in the mixed conifer and ponderosa zones along the moist valley bottoms and edges of the mountain parks. It is also a tall, stately tree, but not as tall or big in diameter as Engelmann spruce. The needles are similar to those of the Engelmann spruce, but are typically covered with a white, silvery, or glaucous bloom; however, this is not always the case. The cones are much larger than Engelmann cones, typically growing to 6 inches in length.

Blue spruce has little lumber value because of its scarcity and its poor quality. It is also of little value to wildlife except as a component of cover. It has found its

Colorado blue spruce

greatest value as a landscape beautification tree. As such, it has been used very widely, not only in our country but in other countries around the world.

Blue spruce is the State tree of both Colorado and Utah.

Colorado blue spruce
(large cone)

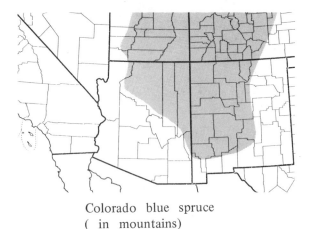

Colorado blue spruce
(in mountains)

PINE FAMILY
(Pinaceae)

Ponderosa pine—*Pinus ponderosa*
"Pino real"

Ponderosa pine covers the major expanse of the forest area of the mountains of the Southwest; thus, it is one of the prime producers of cover for wildlife. Animals which normally occupy the Upper Sonoran Zone find cover as they drift upwards into and through the ponderosa pine zone in summer. Elk and other wild game of the higher mountains move down into this zone for protection in winter. Probably the most typical game of the zone is the Merriam's turkey, which depends upon this forest for food, shelter, and roosting trees. Young trees are browsed by deer, elk, and Barbary sheep. Bears also damage young trees, especially in pine plantations, where they strip the outer bark to get at the inner bark, which they find to their liking.

Squirrels at certain seasons nip off the young tender shoots of older trees, letting them fall to the forest floor. They trim off the terminal fan of needles, then cut off a short length of the small twig that bore the fan. They eat the bark from the twig and drop the stripped twig to the ground. They also shuck the scales from cones to get out the seeds.

Ponderosa pine

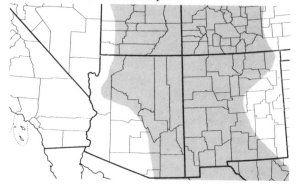

Ponderosa pine

The scientific name of ponderosa pine
is *Pinus ponderosa* . Arizona pine is described
separately. *Pinus* is the classical Latin name
for pine. *Ponderosa* is derived from the Latin
ponderosus, which means ponderous or heavy.
This apparently refers to the large size of the
log, rather than to the heaviness of the wood.
The tree is also frequently called western
yellow pine. It grows on suitable sites throughout the West, from the Black Hills of South
Dakota to California and from Mexico to
Canada, making it the most widely distributed
conifer in North America.

In the Southwest it grows in all the mountain ranges from about 6,500 feet in elevation
to 10,000 feet, even higher in select locations.
It is truly the tree of the Transition Zone, for
it grows on the mountain slopes above the
pigmy forest of pinon-juniper and below the
dark forest of spruce and mixed conifers.

It occurs in association with pinon, juniper, and Gambel oak on the lower portion of
the Zone and with the mixed conifers at the
upper edge. This truly large tree grows from
150 to 180 feet in height and 3 to 5 feet in
diameter. The needles are borne in clusters
of 2 to 3, and they are generally about 5"
long and persist from 3 to 5 years. The
tightly closed, immature cones are green,
changing in the fall to reddish brown as they
ripen. The winged seeds fall soon after the
cones open, and seed may be carried by the
wind for up to 1,000 feet.

The bark on young trees is very dark brown,
brown or nearly black, with small ridges. As
the trees grow older, the ridges become flatter
until the bark is divided into elongated plates,
which are generally yellowish to reddish.
This explains the oft-repeated story that there
are two kinds of this pine, blackjack and
yellow. However, if you could wait that long,
you could see a blackjack pine grow into a
yellow pine in 150 to 200 years.

The pine needles which litter the forest
floor constitute what is known as duff, a
wonderful natural blanket that preserves the
soil and moisture beneath the trees. But at
the same time, where this duff collects heavily it inhibits the growth of grasses and other
plants that would furnish food for game. Open
stands that allow more sunshine to penetrate
to the forest floor are more productive of
game food.

The commercial value of this pine throuh
throughout the western United States is extremely high. New Mexico and Arizona harvest annually about 500 million board-feet
of ponderosa lumber, which is more than is
cut from all the other species of trees put

Ponderosa pine
(bark detail)

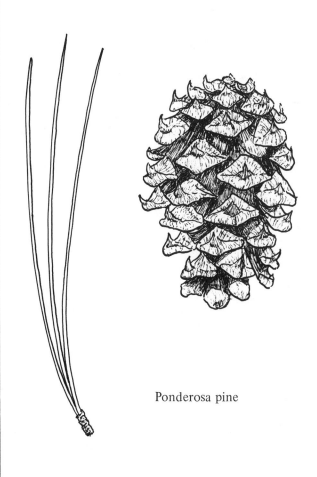

Ponderosa pine

together in these States. More ponderosa pine wood is used for millwork, cabinets, and interior trim in the United States than any other kind. Because of the uniform grain and softness, ponderosa pine is a very fine wood to work with hand tools or power tools.

Ponderosa reproduces readily under certain conditions, especially where mineral soil is exposed. Nursery stock is planted widely throughout its range where natural reproduction fails or is too slow. Thus, this tree lends itself readily to intensive forest management.

PINE FAMILY
(Pinaceae)

Arizona pine—*Pinus ponderosa* var. *Ar arizonica*

A variety of ponderosa pine, known as Arizona pine, occurs in southwestern New Mexico and southeastern Arizona. It is similar to ponderosa except that the needles occur in bundles of 5. It takes close observation to distinguish the two kinds where they are growing in the same general area. The trees are scattered and few in number and are not separated from ponderosa pine in timber harvesting. A grove can be seen in New Mexico along State Road 61 at Rocky Canyon north of Mimbres. In Arizona it may be seen in Chiricahua National Monument.

PINE FAMILY
(Pinaceae)

Chihuahua pine—*Pinus leiophylla* var. *chihuahuana*
"Ocote blanco"

In the scientific name of this pine the word word *leiophylla* refers to flexibility and *chihuahuana* refers to the Mexican State of Chihuahua, an area in which it grows. This pine may be found in southwestern New Mexico and southeastern Arizona north to Navajo County and west to Gile and Pima Counties. It is of limited occurence and of little economic importance. It serves as a limited component of the general forest cover.

Chihuahua pine may be recognized by the small, long-stalked cones that persist on the trees. The cones are smaller than ponderosa cones and are unusual in that they take 3 years to mature. The needles occur 3 in a

Arizona pine
(needles in groups of five)

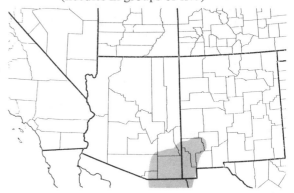

Arizona pine

Largest Chihuahua pine
Portal, Arizona

bundle and are shorter than ponderosa needles. The trees are found scattered among Mexican pinons below the zone of ponderosa pines. The wood is softer and lighter in weight than ponderosa. The sapwood is light straw color, and the heartwood is reddish brown to orange. Working quality is similar to that of ponderosa pine. Specimens can be seen along the Geronimo trail west of Cloverdale, New Mexico, and in the Chiricahua Mountains of Arizona.

Largest Chihuahua pine trunk

Chihuahua pine

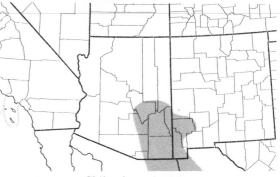

Chihuahua pine

PINE FAMILY
(Pinaceae)

Apache pine—*Pinus engelmannii*

Pinus is the Latin form of the word pine. *Engelmannii* honors George Engelmann, a botanist of St. Louis and an authority on conifers. Apache pine is listed as growing in extreme southwestern New Mexico and in southeastern Arizona in the Chiricahua Mountains. It is more numerous in Mexico. Apache pine is distinguished by its very long needles, the longest of any Southwestern pine and nearly as long as longleaf pine of the southeastern United States. The cone resembles that of ponderosa pine. The trees are generally smaller and more branched than ponderosa pine and are not sufficiently numerous to be of value except as a minor component of game cover.

Apache pines may be seen in the Chiricahua Mountains along Cave Creek and on up into the mountains to Onion Saddle at an elevation of 7,600 feet, where they are displaced by ponderosa pine. On upright growing branches the long needles bend downward, giving a parasol appearance that is quite distinctive. The wood is very resinous and appears to be somewhat coarser grained than that of ponderosa pine.

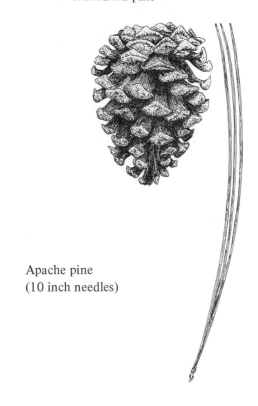

Apache pine
(10 inch needles)

PINE FAMILY
(Pinaceae)

Bristlecone pine—*Pinus aristata*

The specific name refers to the conspicuous bristles on the tips of the cone scales. Bristlecone pine is sometimes called foxtail pine, a name that should be reserved for a similar pine in the high Sierras of California and some mountain tops in Nevada. The needles occur five in a bundle and persist on the branches for many years. This gives the branch the appearance of a foxtail. The needles, besides being short, are characterized by small, white dots of resinous exudation.

This pine occurs at or just below timberline on the highest mountains in New Mexico and Arizona and farther north. Good examples examples can be found on Wheeler Peak and adjacent territory in New Mexico and on the San Francisco Peaks north of Flagstaff, Arizona. In this adverse environment the tree grows quite slowly. They take on very queer shapes where they grow in exposed places. The winter winds and wind-blown snow blast the limbs and bark from the side of the tree exposed to the wind. The tissue continues to grow on the lee side of the tunk, causing the trunk to be oblong in cross-section instead of round as is normal in trees.

Trees well over 1,000 years old have been found in our area. The wood, though not important commercially, is light red in color, lightweight, and not strong. Because it grows slowly, it is fine-grained.

Bristlecone pines over 4,000 years old have been found in California, where they have been called the world's oldest living thing.

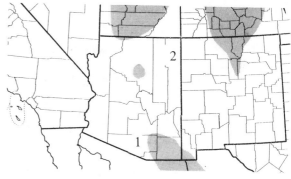

1. Apache pine
2. Bristlecone pine

Bristlecone pine

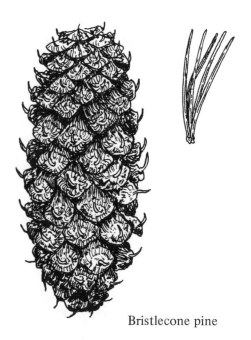

Bristlecone pine

108

PINE FAMILY
(Pinaceae)

Limber pine—*Pinus flexilis*

Flexilis, meaning limber, refers to the limberness of the smaller branches of this pine. The needles, borne in bundles of five, are about 3 inches long. The cones vary from short and broad in northern Colorado to long and slender in New Mexico. Another pine, with similar cones, *Pinus strobiformis*, occurs in the Southwest, and the two species may overlap in distribution in northern New Mexico and southern Colorado. Some authors consider *P. strobiformis* to be a variety of *P. flexilis* and call it *P. flexilis* var. *reflexa*. From my personal observation, I prefer to consider all the pines of this type growing in New Mexico and southern Arizona to be *P. strobiformis* or Mexican white pine.

The seeds of limber pine are large enough to be of value as game feed. The trees occur in the mixed conifer belt and down into the ponderosa pine zone. The wood is yellow to reddish, close-grained, soft, and easily worked.

The tips of the scales of the cones of *P. flexilis* are not recurved, whereas in *P. flexilis* var. *reflexa* they are. It is the latter that has the long, slender cones.

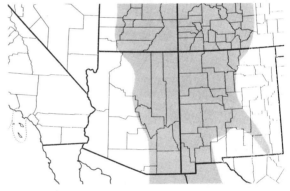

Limber pine

Limber pine
and
Mexican white pine

Limber pine

PINE FAMILY
(Pinaceae)

Mexican white pine—*Pinus strobiformis*

    The specific name refers to a form similar to *strobis*, the specific name of eastern white pine. The cones are generally longer and slimmer than those of the typical limber pine and the tips of the scales are reflexed or turned back. The needles occur in bundles of five and are the same length, generally, as limber pine needles. The trees are generally considered to be taller and straighter than the typical limber pines, which are frequently branched close to the ground and are poor of form. Many of the Mexican white pines are of good enough form to be utilized in lumber manufacture.

    The seeds of this pine are similar to those of limber pine and serve as a source of food for turkeys, squirrels, and other forest animals. The trees occur in the ponderosa pine zone and and up into the mixed conifer zone throughout the higher mountains of the Southwest. The wood is not dissimilar to that of limber pine but may not be so fine-grained.

Mexican white pine

PINE FAMILY
(Pinaceae)

Common pinon—*Pinus edulis*
"Pinon"

    Pinon means the pine with the large nut. The specific name refers to the edible nut. It is found widely spread throughout the Upper Sonoran Zone in New Mexico, Arizona, Utah, southern Colorado and west Texas, and is the State tree of New Mexico. It may occur in pure stands, but is more commonly found mixed with juniper, Gambel oak or, at upper elevations, with ponderosa pine. It is specially characteristic of the breaks around the mesas and on the mesa tops in the elevation range between 5,000 and 7,000 feet.

    Pinon normally grows as a small, many-branched, poorly formed tree, but under good conditions occurs in stands of relatively straight trees up to 50 feet tall. The needles, which are 3/4 to 1½ inches long, are dark green and borne in bundles of 2 or 3, rarely 1, and the bundles are clustered. The small, inconspicuous flowers occur in the spring, and

Common pinon

the cones mature the second year. Good crops of seed occur at intervals of several years. The small, egg-shaped cones are 1½ to 2 inches long and open while on the tree. The wingless seeds are about ½ inch long and edible. The bark is reddish brown and furrowed into scaly ridges.

The pinon nut is highly prized by wildlife, including javelina, deer, wild turkeys, bear, and squirrels. During the autumns of abundant crops, wildlife grows fat on the nuts that literally cover the ground under the heavily bearing trees. The groves of trees also furnish the cover sought by wildlife.

The nuts are also prized by humans, and people from nearby towns and pueblos flock to the woods in the autumn to harvest the seeds, either by shaking them out of the trees onto sheets laid on the ground or by picking them off the bare ground. Local people sell the nuts on the streets, and large quantities are sold through commercial outlets.

The wood is of little commercial value, because of the small size of the trees, but some lumber is cut commercially. The wood is rich in resin and burns with a pleasant odor, making it valuable as fuel for fireplaces. Clear pieces of wood work nicely with hand tools and turn well. Some use is made of the wood locally for posts and poles.

PINE FAMILY
(Pinaceae)

Singleleaf pinon—*Pinus monophylla*
Parry pinon—*Pinus quadrifolia*

Singleleaf pinon, or singleneedle pinon as it is sometimes called, differs from the other pinons in that there is only one needle per bundle. This gives the tree the appearance of having a very thin crop of needles. The species is distributed widely through the mountains of southwest Utah, Nevada, southern California, and northwest Arizona but is not found in New Mexico. It is the State Tree of Nevada.

In general appearance the tree would not readily be distinguished from the other pinons, except for the thinness of the foliage. Closer inspection reveals that there is only 1 needle per bundle rather than 2 or 3 as in Mexican and common pinon or 4 as in Parry pinon.

The nuts are gathered and eaten as are those of the other pinons. The wood is very similar to common pinon.

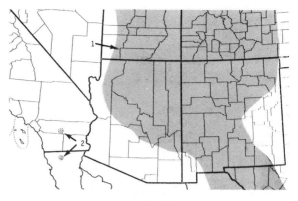

1. Common pinon
2. Parry pinon

Singleleaf pinon

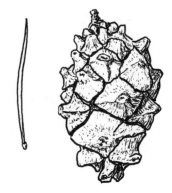

Singleleaf pinon

A fourth species of pinon, Parry or 4-needle pinon grows in a few locations in southern California and adjacent Mexico. Good specimens are said to occur in Santa Rosa Mountains on Toro Peak between Anza-Borrego State Park and Joshua Tree National Monument in southern California.

Parry pinon

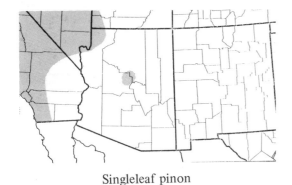

Singleleaf pinon

Parry pinon

Parry pinon

PINE FAMILY
(Pinaceae)

Mexican pinon—*Pinus cembroides*
"Pino pinon"

The scientific name literally means a pine that resembles *Pinus cembra*, the Swiss stone pine. These trees are difficult to distinguish from the common pinon, except that the nuts are generally larger and the shells much harder. The needles are shorter and more often occur in bundles of three. In New Mexico, these trees are confined to the southwest corner of the State from Fort Bayard southward. In Arizona they occur in the southeastern

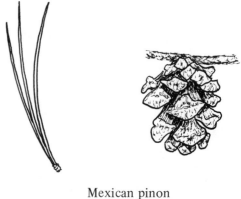

Mexican pinon

112

counties west to Pima and Santa Cruz. Their range extends south into Mexico. The wildlife values are the same as for common pinon, and the wood is not readily distinguished from it.

The trees have been specifically located by the author in the Peloncillo Mountains of Hidalgo County, New Mexico growing in a mixed stand with alligator bark juniper and Chihuahua pines along the Geronimo trail west of Cloverdale. In Arizona they may be observed in the Chiricahua Mountains.

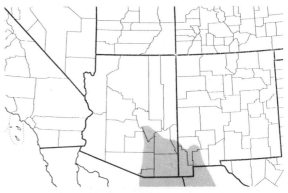

Mexican pinon

PINE FAMILY
(Pinaceae)

Douglas fir—*Pseudotsuga menziesii*

The name Douglas fir is actually a misnomer, since this tree is not a fir. For the same reason, its frequently used common name, red fir, is also a misnomer. The scientific name, *Pseudotsuga menziesii*, is really not as bad as it sounds. *Pseudo* means false and *tsuga* is the generic name given to hemlock; thus, the word means false hemlock. Looking further, the word *tsuga* comes from the Japanese meaning larch. The specific name is in honor of Archibald Menzies, Scotch physician and naturalist.

Douglas fir ranges throughout the forested mountains of the Southwest, where it occurs from about 7500 feet in the lower valleys to just below timberline, but it is most plentiful in the mixed conifer zone between ponderosa pine and the spruce. Here it frequently forms pure stands over wide areas, particularly on north-facing slopes, and may grow in such dense stands that it become stunted. Where growing conditions are good, it becomes a large tree, even for the Southwest. Trees 130 feet or more in height and 3 or more feet in diameter may be found.

The dark green needles are spirally arranged on the branches and are between 3/4 and 1 inch or more in length. They are somewhat flattened and blunt-pointed, whereas spruce needles are angular and sharp. The inconspicuous flowers are orange-red, borne in the spring. The cones are 2½ to 4 inches long and hang down, in contrast to the true fir cones, which grow upright. The cones

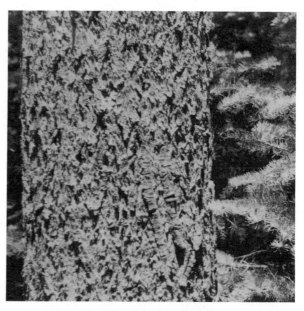

Douglas fir (bark detail)

Douglas fir

are easily identified by the long, 3-pronged bracts that protrude from behind the scales of the cone. In the older trees, the bark becomes as much as 4 to 6 inches thick and is rough, with brown ridges separated by deep furrows. This thick bark makes the trees relatively resistant to damage by light surface fires.

The seeds are readily eaten by grouse, squirrels, and chipmunks, and the leaves are browsed to some extent by mule deer and possibly elk. Otherwise, the chief value for stands of Douglas fir to wildlife is again for cover, as has been mentioned with so many of the tree species. The thick stands of Douglas fir surrounding many of the mountain parks and along the north slopes of the ridges make ideal hiding places for elk and deer.

Commercially, Douglas fir is the second most important species in the Southwest and contributes better than 75 million board-feet of lumber per year to the lumber trade. It is used extensively in the building industry. The wood varies from light yellow to deep pinkish red, orange-red, or deep red in the heartwood, which leads to the name red fir. The wood is not recommended for hobby work, for it has a tendency to split when used in small pieces.

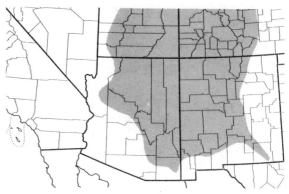
Douglas fir (in mountains)

QUASSIA FAMILY
(Simarubaceae)

Crucifixion-thorn—*Holacantha emoryi*
                Holacantha stewartii
"Corona-de-Cristo"

Holacantha is from Greek words that mean literally wholly thorn. The species names honor men.

The crucifixion-thorn of our area is *H. emoryi. H. stewartii* is mentioned because it occurs in Big Bend National Park in Texas. The common name is also used for various other thorn bushes including *Canotia holacantha* and is sometimes applied to all-thorn, *Koeberlinia spinosa* and other plants.

Our crucifixion-thorn grows in a very limited area in the hottest part of the desert in southwestern Arizona and south into Mexico. A good specimen is said to grow along Highway 80 west of Gila Bend. Other specimens are to be found in the area south of El Centro, and one large one is fenced for added protection. It is now illegal to cut this plant in Arizona.

Crucifixion-thorn

114

This plant is leafless. The green stems serve the function of green leaves. The small flowers are borne among the branches. The fruits are borne in large clusters like maize, tan colored, and long-lasting. The wood is said to be golden molasses color with beautiful natural luster. The wood is hard and heavy and polishes nicely. The plant grows as a large shrub up to 15 feet high. It is too rare to be of any value except as a botanical oddity.

Stewart crucifixion-thorn is said to be more low-growing, spreading out over small sand dunes that develop at the base. Otherwise, it is very similar.

Crucifixion-thorn

QUASSIA FAMILY
(Simarubaceae)

Tree of heaven—*Ailanthus altissima*

Ailanthus is from a Chinese word meaning tree of heaven, referring to its height. *Altissima* also means very tall. In our area it is hard to see why either name applies.

This plant was introduced from China and and can probably be classed as naturalized, as it is found in southern New Mexico in places where it is not likely that it was planted. It spreads from both seeds and root suckers. It has been used widely as an ornamental and its spreading habit is objectionable. It is included in this publication because it has become so widespread.

The compound leaves have as many as 41 leaflets but generally fewer. The leaflets are generally about 3 to 5 inches long and pointed at the tip. The flowers appear as large, loose terminal clusters, yellowish in color. The fruits are samaras similar to those of ash, but are borne in large dense clusters. The wood is light yellow to golden brown, very light and soft, coarse, and open-grained. It could be used where strength is not important.

This tree may be found as an ornamental in towns and around homesites throughout our area.

ROSE FAMILY
(Rosaceae)

Utah serviceberry—*Amelanchier utahensis*
Saskatoon or common serviceberry—
    A. alnifolia
Mountain serviceberry (syn. A. utahensis)—
    A. oreophila
Serviceberry (syn. A. utahensis)—*A. goldmanii*
Serviceberry (syn. A. utahensis)—*A. bakeri*

The genus name is derived from the French name of a European species, *alnifolia* means alder-leaved, from the leaf shape, *oreophila* means mountain loving, and the last two honor men.

Utah serviceberry occurs in the mountainous part of New Mexico, except in the far southern part, and across the central and northeastern part of Arizona and northward. It is generally found as a bushy shrub seldom over 4 or 5 feet tall, but may become larger. It is commonly found among rocks or on steep hillsides. Heavy browsing by game accounts for the more common bushy form. The 5-petaled, white flowers are borne in small clusters on the ends of small branches. The tiny, apple-like fruits are about ¼ inch in diameter, bluish-black and juicy when ripe. The leaves are nearly round with finely serrated edges. The fruits are edible and were used in various ways by pioneer women. One common name for the plant is pemmicanbush because the berries were used in making pemmican. The wood is hard and heavy. The nearly white sapwood has a pinkish cast, and the heart is light reddish brown. Deer browse the plants, and birds make extensive use of the berries.

Saskatoon, or common serviceberry, as it is sometimes called, is very widespread in the Rocky Mountain west, but its range in our area is limited to the northern mountains of New Mexico and northward. The flowers and seeds of this species are similar to Utah serviceberry, but the leaves are larger and shaped more like alder leaves, about 2 inches long and oval or rounded with flattened or rounded tips. The plant form is apt to be more open-growing with fewer stems to a clump, and the stems taller. It also is subject to heavy grazing pressure that may keep it in a more rounded form.

Mountain serviceberry has limited range in our area but is listed as occurring at Capital Reef National Monument in Utah and at Walnut Canyon National Monument in Arizona. Arizona. It is a low, hairy-leafed shrub that grows in clumps.

Utah serviceberry

Utah serviceberry

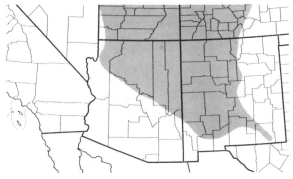

Utah serviceberry
(including synonyms)

116

Goldman serviceberry is listed as occurring occurring at the Grand Canyon. Its range is said to include northwestern New Mexico.

Baker serviceberry is listed for Canyon de Chelly and Walnut Canyon National Monument in Arizona, and for southern Colorado. The leaves are pubescent on both sides, deeply notched around the tip; the flowers are small.

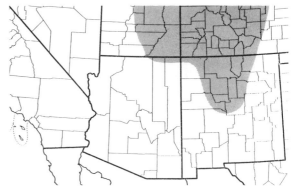

Common serviceberry

ROSE FAMILY
(Rosaceae)

True mountainmahogany—*Cercocarpus*
"Palo duro"   *montanus*
Hairy mountainmahogany—*C. breviflorus*
Birchleaf mountainmahogany—*C. betuloides*
Curlleaf mountainmahogany—*C. ledifolius*
Arizona mountainmahogany—*C. arizonica*
Littleleaf mountainmahogany—*C. intricatus*

True mountainmahogany

In treating the mountainmahoganies, one may list all of the above species or he may follow F. L. Martin and list only one, *C. montanus*, and a few varieties of that species. Since common usage has accepted at least the first four species listed, I have chosen to list all six compiled by various botanists for the Southwestern national monuments and parks.

The generic name comes from *kerkos*, a Greek word for tail, and *karpos* for fruit, thus tailed fruit, alluding to the long tail attached to the fruiting body of this plant. *Montanus* refers to the fact that this is a mountain plant; *breviflorus* means short-flowered; *betuloides* refers to the birchlike leaves; *ledifolius* means curled leaf; *intricatus* refers to the intricate branching.

True mountainmahogany, as I have considered it, occurs across northern New Mexico in the mountainous areas and south through the Sacramento Mountains. It probably occurs in northeastern Arizona and southeastern Utah, and the range extends northward through Colorado. This species is generally only a bush, up to 10 feet high, with slender stems. Mountainmahogany can be recognized readily when in fruit by the long, silvery-haired tails attached to the fruits. The ½-inch-long seed is attached to the tail at the tip. The leaves are about 1 inch long and ½ inch wide, notched near the apex, and with distinct veins. The sapwood is light straw

True mountainmahogany

117

color and the heartwood in an old mature stem is deep red and very hard and heavy. A synonym for this species is *C. parvifolius*.

Hairy mountainmahogany occurs in the mountains of southern and central New Mexico and southeast and central Arizona, south into Mexico. This species is usually a large shrub, but in the Animas Mountains of southwest New Mexico I saw a tree at least 1 foot in diameter and 20 feet tall. Other quite large logs have been reported to me from the Organ Mountains. The seed tails are about 1½ inches long, otherwise the characteristics are much like true mountainmahogany. The sapwood is light straw color and the heartwood in large trunks is deep, mahogany red, very hard, heavy, and dense. It makes beautiful turned objects.

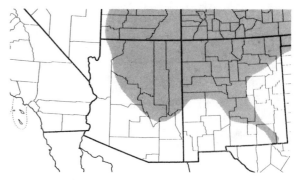

True mountainmahogany

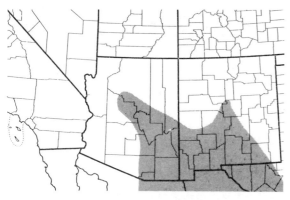

Hairy mountainmahogany

Birchleaf mountainmahogany occurs in Arizona, Oregon, California, and Mexico, but not in New Mexico. In Arizona it occurs in the chaparral zone in the center of the State. The botanical characteristics are very similar to the other mountainmahoganies. It occurs as a large shrub or small tree to 20 feet tall and several inches in diameter.

Hairy mountainmahogany

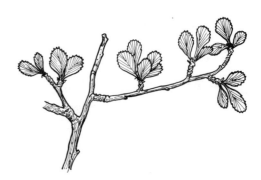

Birchleaf mountainmahogany

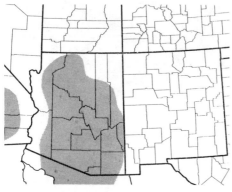

Birchleaf mountainmahogany

Curlleaf mountainmahogany does not occur in New Mexico. In Arizona it is known from the country around the Grand Canyon. It is found from southwestern Colorado and north to Montana, west to Washington, and south to southern California. The leaves in this species are ½ to 1¼ inches long and 3/8 inches wide with edges rolled under, thick, and leathery. The edges are smooth. It occurs as small trees, often in clumps. The wood is pink with white sapwood.

Curlleaf mountainmahogany

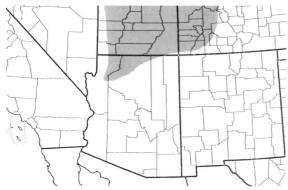

Curlleaf mountainmahogany

Arizona mountainmahogany has been reported from the area around the Grand Canyon. It occurs in central Utah, Nevada, and northern Arizona. The shrub is spiny and of small size. The leaves are only about half as long as those of curlleaf and so tightly curled they appear to be linear.

Littleleaf mountainmahogany is similar to Arizona mountainmahogany but extends on into California. These last two species are considered to be one and the same by some browse experts.

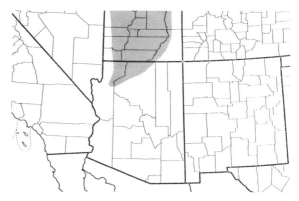

Arizona mountainmahogany

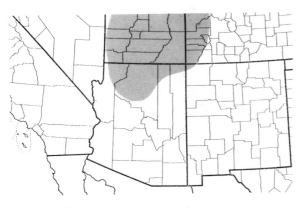

Littleleaf mountainmahogany

Littleleaf mountainmahogany

ROSE FAMILY
(Rosaceae)

Stansbury cliffrose—*Cowania stansburiana*

Cowania honors an English merchant who introduced various American plants into England, and the species name honors botanist Stansbury. Cliffrose reaches its best development in Arizona and Utah. It extends into the far western edge of New Mexico only sparingly. In New Mexico, this evergreen plant is only a small shrub, but in northern Arizona and Utah it becomes a poorly shaped tree to about 20 feet tall and up to 6 inches in diameter.

The very small leaves are thick, with 3 to 7 points, stiff, and leathery. They are somewhat similar to bitterbrush, but thicker. The flowers are borne singly, up to 1 inch across and numerous. Five or more seeds develop in a cluster, each with a long, feathery white tail up to 2 inches long. The wood is quite hard and dense and cross-grained. The spring wood is very light tan, and the summer wood is brown, giving a pleasing grain pattern.

Cliffrose is a very valuable browse plant in its range. It is so heavily browsed by deer and domestic stock that it is often hard to find a well-developed plant. This situation develops in many of the most palatable browse species so that the true form of the plant may seldom be seen. Ceanothus, fendler bush, mountainmahogany, bitterbrush, skunkbush in some areas, and Wright's silktassel are a few of the plants subject to this severe hedging.

Stansbury cliffrose

Stansbury cliffrose

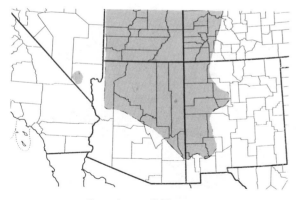

Stansbury cliffrose

ROSE FAMILY
(Rosaceae)

Blackbrush—*Coleogyne ramosissima*

Coleogyne means sheathed ovary, from Greek *koloes*, sheath, and *gyne*, female. The specific name is a Latin word meaning very intricately branched. This shrub is intricately branched, with numerous side branches at right angles to the main stems and many armed branchlets at right angles to the side branches.

This shrub occurs in southern Nevada, Utah, southwestern Colorado, and Arizona and to the Mohave Desert region of southern California, but not in New Mexico. It ranges through a belt overlapping the northern and southern deserts. The small yellow flowers occur solitary at the ends of the short branchlets. The fruits are borne solitary with a twisted threadlike stalk from one side and conspicuous, dense hairs at the base of the stalk. The small opposite or crowded leaves are narrowly club-shaped with 3 or 5 lobes at the top. The stems become black with age.

The plant furnishes browse for domestic stock and it is utilized by deer, but it is considered to be a range pest. It occurs in fairly dense stands in northern Arizona and southern Utah on gravelly soils. Well developed plants may be seen around Moab, Utah.

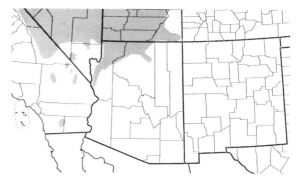
Blackbrush

ROSE FAMILY
(Rosaceae)

River hawthorn—*Crataegus rivularis*
Fireberry hawthorn—*C. chrysocarpa*
Cerro hawthorn—*C. erythropoda*
Wooton hawthorn—*C. wootoniana*
"Tejocote" or "texocotl"

These four hawthorns are listed as occurring in our area, in contrast to the very large number of hawthorns occurring in Texas and east. *Crataegus* is from Greek *krataigos*, strong, and refers to the strong wood. *Rivularis* means growing by a river, and *chrysocarpa* means yellow-seeded. *Erythropoda* literally means red-footed. *Wootoniana* honors an early New Mexico botanist by the name of Wooton.

The hawthorns are scarce in our area. The four species here listed are recorded for New Mexico, but only two occur in Arizona. Wooton hawthorn is listed only for the Sacra-

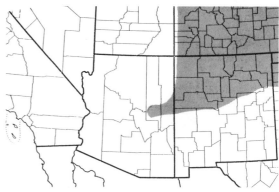
River hawthorn

River hawthorn

mento and Mogollon Mountains of central and southwestern New Mexico. Fireberry hawthorn is widely spread from Canada, south to New Mexico, but not in Arizona. River hawthorn occurs in the mountains of north-central New Mexico and has been reported from as far west as Winslow, Arizona. Cerro hawthorn occurs in northeastern New Mexico and has been reported in the White Mountains and Oak Creek Canyon in Arizona.

All the hawthorns are well-armed with sharp spines. The flowers are white. The cerro fruit is orange or red, and river hawthorn fruit is bluish-black; all resemble rose hips. The leaves are irregular in outline with toothed edges. The river hawthorn is probably the largest, often occurring in clumps with individual stems to 20 or more feet in height and 6 to 8 inches in diameter. The wood of the river hawthorn has light straw to white sapwood, lined with brown. The heartwood is deep brown in mature trees. The wood is heavy, hard, and cross-grained. None of these shrubs is plentiful enough to be of much value to wildlife, although some value is accredited to river hawthorn.

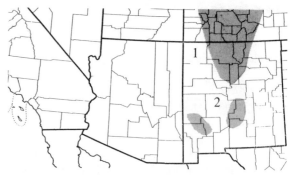

1. Fireberry hawthorn
2. Wooton hawthorn

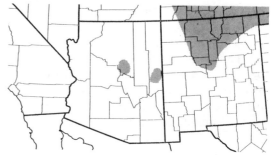

Cerro hawthorn

ROSE FAMILY
(Rosaceae)

Shrubby cinquefoil—*Dasiphora fruticosa*
            or *Potentilla fruticosa*

Some authors place our shrubby cinquefoil in the genus *Dasiphora* and some in the genus *Potentilla*. There are many other species of *Potentilla*, but they are not true shrubs. *Potentilla* comes from *potens*, meaning powerful, and refers to the medicinal value. *Fruticosa* means shrubby, referring to the growth habit of the plant. *Dasiphora* is from Greek, meaning dense and shaggy, and refers to the hairy seeds.

This is a very wide-ranging shrub. It occurs all across North America and into Europe and Asia. In our area it appears in the high mountains of New Mexico and eastern Arizona, and in southern Colorado at elevations up to 10,000 feet. It is a low bushy shrub that occurs in dense stands in open, high mountain meadows. It is covered with bright yellow flowers through much of the summer season. The finely cut leaves are compound with as many as 7 leaflets, and

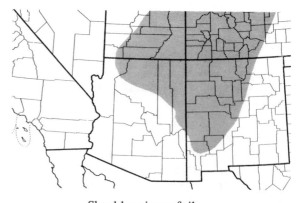

Shrubby cinquefoil
(in high mountains)

122

hairy. The bark of the stems becomes shreddy with age. The forage is rated poor for domestic stock but is used lightly by deer and elk. It occurs so high in the mountains that it is seldom available for winter feed.

The shrub has been domesticated and several horticultural varieties are propagated for landscaping.

ROSE FAMILY
(Rosaceae)

Apacheplume—*Fallugia paradoxa*
"Ponil"

Fallugia honors an early Italian botanist. *Paradoxa*, according to one source, refers to the flower's paradoxical resemblance to roses. The name may also derive from the fact that when this species was originally placed in the genus *Sieversia*, it was the only shrub in that genus.

Apacheplume occurs throughout our area from about 5,000 feet to 7,500 or to 8,000 feet in northern New Mexico. It frequently occurs along the sides of dry washes and wherever it gets extra moisture, but is also found on dry hillsides. It tends to grow in clumps with the bushes 6 feet tall or less. The roselike white flowers are showy in the early summer, but the feathery clusters of plumrose fruits, white to pinkish in the fall and winter, are even more showy. These plumes give the bush its common name. The leaves are very small, generally with 3 points, partially evergreen, and crowded on the stems. They might be mistaken for cliffrose but are not as thick. Generally, the bush is not heavily used by game or stock but may be in selected locations. The stems seldom exceed an inch in diameter, and the older ones are covered with shreddy bark.

Apacheplume

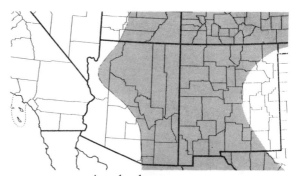

Apacheplume
(in high mountains)

Apacheplume

123

ROSE FAMILY
(Rosaceae)

Rockspirea—*Holodiscus dumosus*

Rockspirea is often called oceanspray, but that name should be reserved for *H. discolor* on the Pacific coast. *Holodiscus* comes from *holo*, meaning entire, and *diskos* or disk, thus a flower with an entire disk. *Dumosus* is from Latin *dumus*, meaning bramble.

This is another shrub that occurs widely throughout our area in the ponderosa pine zone of the higher mountains and up into the mixed conifer zone. It is most often found in moister sites. It grows larger in the southern mountains where I have found it up to 8 feet tall and with stems nearly 2 inches in diameter, but is usually somewhat smaller. The flowers occur in terminal clusters up to 2 inches long, creamy white, with the individual blooms very small. The leaves are about 1½ inches long, pointed at the base, and sawtooth notched around the upper ½ to the tip. The veins are prominent and small scalelike leaflets are attached at the base of the short stems. The shrub has little value but has been reported as used by deer. The wood is creamy white, dense, and fine-grained.

ROSE FAMILY
(Rosaceae)

Squawapple—*Peraphyllum ramosissimum*

In the genus name, *pera* means excessively and *phyllon* means leaf, thus very leafy. The species name refers to the intricate branching.

Squawapple is found along the northern border of New Mexico, where it extends into the State from the north. The shrub is showy in bloom. The 5-petaled, white to pink flowers occur in racemes of 2 to 3 and are up to ½ inch across. The small apple-like fruits are yellow with pink or reddish cheeks and bitter to the taste. The simple, alternate leaves are clustered at the ends of the stubby, intricately branched limbs. The shrub is generally low-growing. The limbs are too small to use for wood.

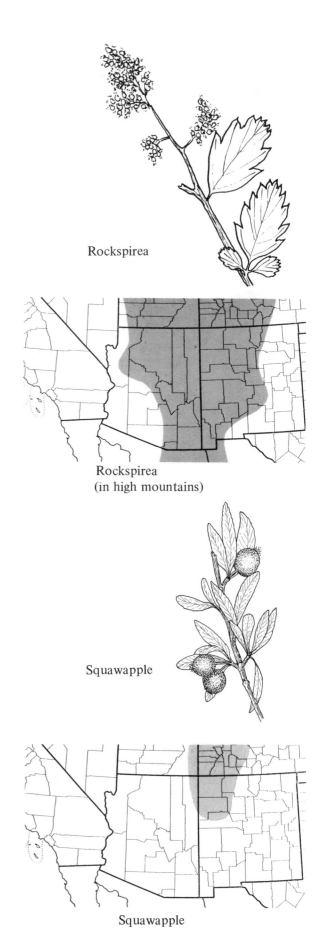

Rockspirea

Rockspirea
(in high mountains)

Squawapple

Squawapple

ROSE FAMILY
(*Rosaceae*)

Mountain ninebark—*Physocarpus monogynus*
Ninebark—*Physocarpus malvaceus*

Physa means bladder; *karpos*, fruit; thus, inflated fruit. *Monogynus* means solitary pistil.

Ninebark is a low western shrub to 3 feet high. It occurs in the south-central and Sangre de Cristo Mountains of New Mexico and west into Arizona. The small white to pink flowers are clustered at the ends of the branches. The individual blooms are very small, 5-petaled. The simple, alternate leaves are palmately lobed with 3 to 5 shallow lobes per leaf. The leaves are small. The plant is quite showy in bloom. It has little wildlife value but has been reported to be eaten by deer.

Physocarpus malvaceus is reported from Capital Reef National Park in Utah.

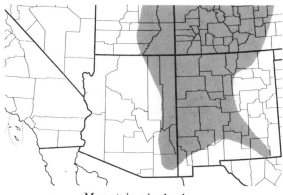

Mountain ninebark

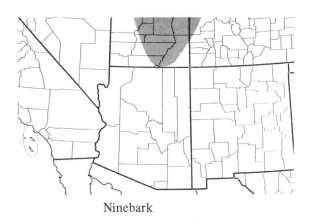

Ninebark

ROSE FAMILY
(*Rosaceae*)

Black western chokecherry—*Prunus virginiana*
     var. *melanocarpa*
Southwestern chokecherry—*P. virens*
Gila chokecherry—*P. serotina* var. *rufula* or
     P. virens var. rufula

The nomenclature for cherries of the Southwest is very much confused. No two authors agree, and I have decided to change my earlier assessment of the situation. I have based my classification on tree form, fruit size, geographical distribution, and a study of the literature.

The chokecherry common to the north and east of our region is *P. virginiana*. Elbert Little calls our typical northern chokecherry by this name, but other authors have seen fit to give it the variety designation of *melano-carpa*, meaning black fruit. The Southwestern chokecherry is listed by Little as *P. virens*, but under this he includes the Gile chokecherry. There is a chokecherry that grows in the Black Range of New Mexico which has a much different growth habit than the typical common chokecherry. This I refer to as *P. virens*. The Gila chokecherry I call *P. serotina* var. *rufula*

Black western chokecherry

125

or *P. virens* var. *rufula* is definitely a tree cherry with a single trunk and not clump forming. This tree is found in far southwestern New Mexico and in southeastern Arizona where I saw good examples in the Cave Creek area of the Chiricahua Mountains.

Virens means greening and refers to the half-evergreen leaves. *Rufula* is red, for the color of the fruit. *Serotina* means late flowering.

The black western chokecherry grows in the moist northern mountain valleys and along the watercourses on the adjoining plains. In New Mexico it occurs in the western 2/3 and northeast, and in Arizona in the northeastern 1/3 and to the rim of the Grand Canyon. In one variety or another, it occurs north, west, and east across the continent.

The small trees or large shrubs are up to about 20 feet tall and seldom more than a few inches in diameter. The stems are generally crooked and occur in clumps. The flowers occur in early spring in long racemes, white in color. The fruit is dark red or nearly black when ripe, small and round, juicy and quite astringent. The bark is generally smooth, dark brown and somewhat rough in older trees. The wood is hard, heavy, and light brown, with a greenish cast between the heart and light-colored sapwood.

The southwestern chokecherry I know from the Black Range in New Mexico is also clump forming, but the individual trees appear to be straighter, with the stems of the clump coming from a common center. The leaves appear to be larger but the fruit is small like the the black western chokecherry. Otherwise, the characteristics are about the same.

The Gila chokecherry is truly a tree, as has been mentioned. The trees have a tendency to lean but may grow to a foot in diameter and 25 to 30 feet tall. The old trunks are covered with bark that has broken into plates, giving it a very distinctive appearance. The leaves are smaller than other chokecherries so that the crown appears thin. The cherries, on the other hand, are the largest of our chokecherries, often ½ inch in diameter. The wood is similar to eastern black cherry, reddish brown and hard.

All the chokecherries are relished by wildlife, including songbirds, band-tailed pigeons, grouse, wild turkeys, fox, bear, and other furbearers. The leaves are browsed by deer, elk, and probably antelope. The chokecherries are used locally in making wine, jams, and jellies. The leaves, under some circumstances, are poisonous to livestock.

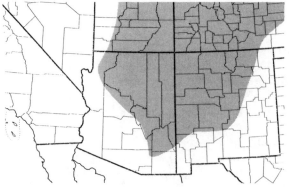

Black western chokecherry

Southwestern chokecherry

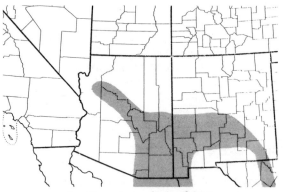

Southwestern chokecherry

Gila chokecherry

126

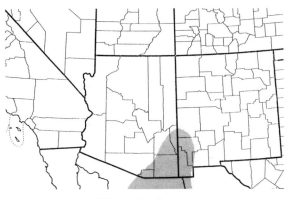

Gila chokecherry

ROSE FAMILY
(Rosaceae)

Bitter cherry—*Prunus emarginata*

Emarginata refers to the shallow notch at the leaf apex. The bitter cherry occurs in southwestern New Mexico, southeastern and central Arizona and on north to British Columbia. It grows to a small tree up to about 25 feet in height and several inches in diameter. It is distinguished from choke-cherries by the fact that its flowers are in small clusters of 3 or 4 and that the fruit is acid and bitter. The wood is softer and more brittle than chokecherry; the heartwood is light tan to medium brown in color, streaked with green. Like all the cherry woods it has an odor similar to that of the crushed leaves. None of our cherry or plum woods have any commercial value.

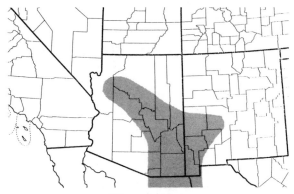

Bitter cherry

ROSE FAMILY
(Rosaceae)

Wild plum—*Prunus americana*

Prunus is the Latin name for plum, and the specific name needs no explanation. This is the only plum native to our region. It does not occur native in Arizona, and in New Mexico it is limited to the northeast and central mountains. It occurs around Farmington in the northwest but perhaps by introduction. It now grows abundantly along fences and ditches in the fields of mountain valleys. It is no longer possible to differentiate between bushes that are truly wild and ones that have been planted by homesteaders and settlers who wanted the plums for domestic use.

The trees are covered with white flowers in early spring. The leaves are 2 to 4 inches long, with sharply saw-toothed edges and a wrinkled appearance. The trees or large shrubs are about 10 feet tall and generally form thickets that make good escape cover for rabbits and birds. The wood is hard, heavy, and difficult to work. It has a rich brown color with a distinct pattern caused by the lighter brown spring wood and the darker summer wood.

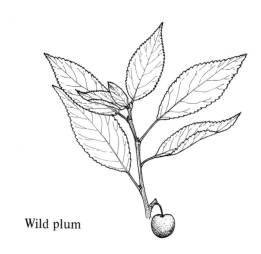

Wild plum

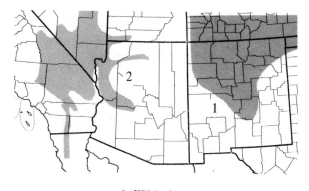

1. Wild plum
2. Desert almond

ROSE FAMILY
(Rosaceae)

Desert apricot—*Prunus fremontii*
Desert peach—*Prunus andersonii*
Desert almond—*Prunus fasciculata*

Prunus is the Latin name for plum. *Fremontii* honors the explorer, no doubt, and *fasciculata* refers to the fasciculate arrangement of the leaves near the ends of the branche branches. *Andersonii* honors Edgar Anderson, American botanist.

There is some confusion in the literature regarding desert almond, desert peach, and desert apricot. According to Benson and Darrow, desert peach occurs farther north in California, beyond the scope of this book. Desert almond occurs in southwestern Utah, southern Nevada, western Arizona, and southern California, while desert apricot occurs along the western edge of the Salton Sea basin in southeastern California. Desert almond has been planted in other areas of the Southwest in an effort to improve game ranges. It is distinguished from the apricot by the lack of any fleshy fruit around the pit. The covering cracks open, exposing the pit. The apricot has a thin layer of edible flesh over the pit. Both have white flowers, in contrast to the pink flowers of desert peach.

All 3 plants occur as shrubs about 4 to 6 feet in height or perhaps taller on good sites. The stems grow to about 2 inches in diameter. The wood is hard, cross-grained, and light brown in color, or white in desert almond.

Desert almond

ROSE FAMILY
(Rosaceae)

Antelope bitterbrush—*Purshia tridentata*

Purshia honors an early German botanist who collected in America. *Tridentata* refers to the 3 indentations at the apex of the leaf. The plant occurs in far northwestern New Mexico, Arizona, north to Montana and west to California. Because its range is limited in our area, it is not as important here as it is farther north. It occurs generally as a low shrub but in protected places and on favorable sites may become almost treelike with a trunk a few inches in diameter and a total height of about 10 feet.

Antelope bitterbush

The yellow, 5-petaled flowers are borne singly. Single, black, small fruits about the size of a grain of wheat develop and just before before ripening are filled with a black juice. Upon ripening, the fruits fall very quickly to the ground, making it difficult to gather seeds in economical quantities. Where larger stems develop, the wood is light-brown in color, very hard, heavy, and cross-grained.

This is another of the shrubs that is so very valuable as browse for livestock and deer. It is so heavily used that it is seldom possible to find a well-developed plant. I have seen whole hillsides in Idaho where the brush has been killed from heavy winter use by deer.

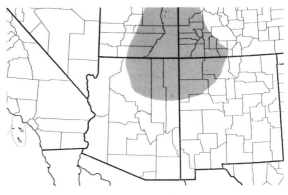

Antelope bitterbush

ROSE FAMILY
(Rosaceae)

Prickly rose—*Rosa acicularis*
Arizona rose—*Rosa arizonica*
Arkansas rose—*Rosa arkansana*
Fendler rose—*Rosa woodsii* var. *fendleri*
Pale-leaf rose—*Rosa hypoleuca*
New Mexico rose—*Rosa neomexicana*
Nootka rose—*Rosa nutkana*
Standley rose—*Rosa standleyi*
Desert rose—*Rosa stellata*
Woods' rose—*Rosa woodsii*
"Rosas"

The above ten species of rose have been reported for our area and there may well be more. Some references list *R. manca* but that is a synonym for *R. nutkana.* It would require full botanical descriptions of each rose, along with identification keys, to make it possible to identify all these roses in the field, and that is beyond the scope of this publication. *Rosa* is Latin for rose.

In the name for prickly rose, *acicularis* refers to the numerous prickles. *Rosa sayi* is another name for this rose. This is a wide-spread species occurring from New Mexico northward to Alaska and east to New York. The beautiful pink flowers, as much as 2 inches across, occur on old wood. The bush is gen-erally about 3 feet tall.

Arizona rose is named for Arizona and occurs in the ponderosa pine zone in the mountains of New Mexico and Arizona. This is a small shrub bearing small, pink roses.

Arkansas rose was named for the Arkansas River, on the banks of which it was

Wild rose

found. It occurs in New Mexico and northward through Colorado to elevations of 9,000 feet. The plant grows about 1½ feet tall with very bristly and prickly stems. The flowers are about 1½ to 2 inches across.

Fendler rose probably honors German botanist August Fendler. It occurs quite widely spread in Arizona from the Saguaro National Monument to the Grand Canyon.

Hypoleuca, the species name for pale-leaf rose, literally means pale, referring to the underside of the leaf. This rose was first collected near Winston, New Mexico, but extends into Arizona. The bush becomes about 3 feet tall and bright pink flowers are large.

New Mexico rose occurs in the Transition and Canadian Zones of southern Colorado, south into New Mexico and west through Arizona.

Nutkana is the Latin form of Nootka, from Nootka Sound in British Columbia. This is a large shrub, up to 5 feet, with pink to white roses up to 3 inches across. It occurs from New Mexico, northward through the Rocky Mountains at altitudes from 3,500 to 10,000 feet.

Standley rose was named for Paul C. Standley, an American botanist. This type specimen was collected near Pecos, New Mexico. It is a bush about 3 feet tall with white to pink flowers.

Desert or star rose, *R. stellata*, is named for its stellate hairs. It forms a medium-sized bush about 2 feet tall with rose-purple flowers, and occurs at about 8,500 feet in New Mexico and west into Arizona.

Woods' rose is named for Joseph Woods, an English student of the genus. Fendler rose is sometimes given as a variety of Woods' rose. This rose is one of the largest of the wild roses, growing to 6 feet tall with pink roses about 2 inches across. It is widely spread through New Mexico and Arizona, north to Canada.

Roses of one species or another occur throughout the mountains of our area. Distribution maps are not available.

ROSE FAMILY
(Rosaceae)

Alice raspberry—*Rubus aliceae*
Arizona dewberry—*R. arizonensis*
Similar raspberry—*R. exrubicundus*
Bristly raspberry—*R. hispidus*
"Zarzamora"
Whitebark raspberry—*R. leucodermis*
New Mexico raspberry—*R. neomexicana*
Western thimbleberry—*R. parviflorus*
American red raspberry—*R. strigosus*

Robert A. Vines points out that to cover the genus *Rubus* adequately would require a monograph. He lists 60 species for the Southwest, which for him included Texas. Many species occur in only one county. I have chosen the species that have been reported from the parks, monuments, and national forests of our area. My list includes 1 thimbleberry, 2 dewberries, and 5 raspberries. No blackberries are listed for our area.

Alice raspberry is named for Alice Eastwood. This is an erect bramble armed with prickles rather than bristles. It has been reported from Santa Fe Canyon, near Santa Fe, New Mexico.

Arizona dewberry has widespread occurrence from Texas, through New Mexico and Arizona. It is a trailing bramble that is very prickly.

Similar raspberry gets its name from the resemblance to *R. rubicundus*. It is an upright and unarmed raspberry with small, dry, red fruit from south-central New Mexico, west into Arizona.

Bristly dewberry is listed as occurring at Capital Reef National Monument. *Hispidus* refers to the bristly character of the plant. Whitebark raspberry is reported from New Mexico but is usually a more northern species. It has large, arching canes which root at the tips. The fruit is dark purple or black or sometimes red.

New Mexico raspberry ranges through the high mountains of New Mexico, Arizona, and south into Mexico. It is a large, upright plant, unarmed. It produces large red raspberries.

Parviflorus is the name of western thimbleberry and means small flowered. It occurs from the mountains of Mexico, through the high mountains of New Mexico, north to Canada. The plant grows to 6 feet in height with very large leaves, up to 12 inches broad and only moderately lobed. The fruits are red and large and good to eat in areas of adequate moisture. The stems are unarmed.

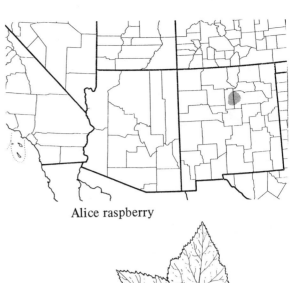

Alice raspberry

Arizona dewberry

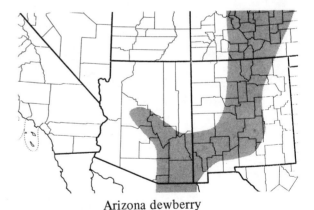

Arizona dewberry

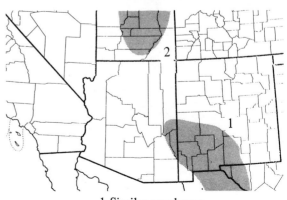

1. Similar raspberry
2. Bristly raspberry

American red raspberries are stiff-bristled, and *stirgosus* means just that. This raspberry is widely spread throughout North America and in our area occurs in both New Mexico and Arizona and northward in higher and drier sites. The red fruits have few divisions and they are apt to fall apart in picking.

All the species named have more or less showy flowers, white in color, appearing in the spring and early summer. The fruit ripens in the summer and early fall. People can often be seen gathering it along roadsides. All these species are of value to wildlife and are used by deer for browse and by bears, other mammals, and birds for the fruit. They also make fine cover for small wildlife.

Western thimbleberry

American red raspberry

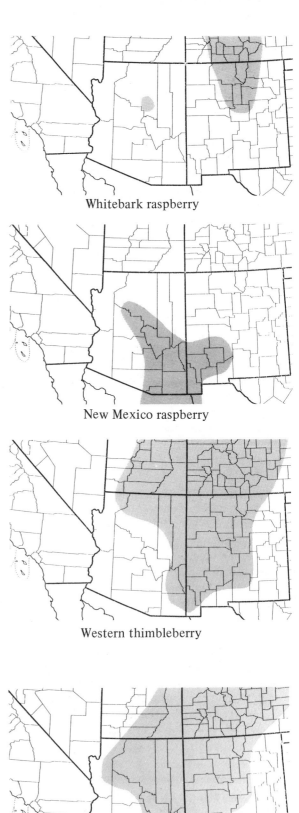

Whitebark raspberry

New Mexico raspberry

Western thimbleberry

American red raspberry

ROSE FAMILY
(Rosaceae)

Arizona mountainash—*Sorbus dumosa*
Green mountainash—*Sorbus scopulina*
Elderleaf mountainash—*Sorbus sambucifolius*

Sorbus is the Latin name for the genus, and *dumosa* refers to the shrubby character of the plant. *Scopulina* means rocklike, and *sambucifolius* no doubt refers to the elder-like leaves.

Arizona mountainash ranges through the high mountains of New Mexico and Arizona at elevations from 7,500 to 10,000 feet, in the open forests. It is a slender shrub to 15 feet tall. The leaves are odd, pinnately compound with up to 15 leaflets, each leaflet long and slender. The flowers are white and borne in large rounded clusters at the ends of the branches. The clusters of small berry-like fruits are showy. The seeds make good feed for birds and other wildlife.

Green mountainash occurs in the central and northern mountains of New Mexico, north-ward to Canada, and west to Arizona. It is also a plant of the high mountain forests. The flower heads are more flat-topped than those in Arizona mountainash. This is a stouter appearing shrub than the Arizona species, but otherwise the botanical characteristics are very much the same.

The third species is reported from the Grand Canyon in Arizona.

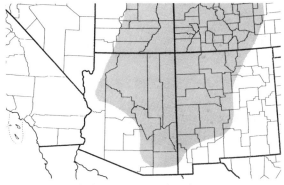
Arizona mountainash

Green mountainash

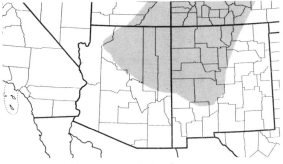
Green mountainash

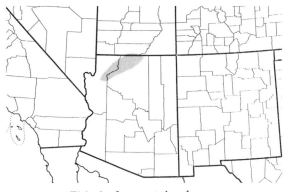
Elderleaf mountainash

ROSE FAMILY
(Rosaceae)

Torrey vauquelinia—*Vauquelinia californica*

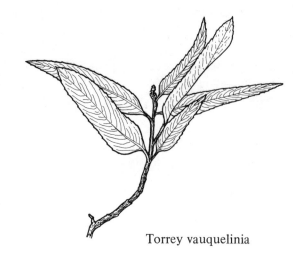

Torrey vauquelinia

In this plant, the genus name honors Louis Vauquelin, a French chemist. It is often referred to as Arizona rosewood because of the color of the wood. The sapwood is straw colored and the heartwood varies from light brown through bright red to deep brown. It is cross-grained, very hard, heavy, and difficult to carve but worth the effort for making small articles.

This evergreen plant occurs in southwestern Texas, northern Mexico, perhaps in extreme southwest New Mexico, and in southeastern and south-central Arizona. It can be seen on a limestone hill on the road from Douglas, Arizona, to Guadalupe Canyon in southwest New Mexico, and on Mount Lemmon near Tucson at about the 4,000-foot level. It is usually found as a large shrub or small tree about 10 to 15 feet high and 6 inches in diameter but is reported to grow larger. The leaves are about ¼ inch wide and up to 4 inches long with edges serrated. They are leathery and yellowish green. The flowers are small and white, in small clusters. The seed capsule is only about ¼ inch long and remains attached through the winter.

One botanist considers the *Vauguelina* found near Douglas, Arizona to be a separate species, *V. pauciflora.*

Torrey vauquelinia

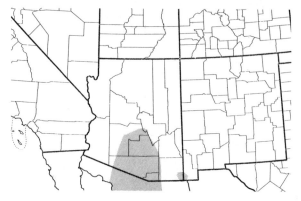

Torrey vauquelinia

134

RUE FAMILY
(Rutaceae)

Narrowleaf hoptree—*Ptelea angustifolia*
Pale hoptree—*Ptelea pallida*
Common hoptree—*Ptelea trifoliata*
"Cola de Zorrillo"

The genus name is the Greek name for elm; *angustifolia* means narrow-leafed; *pallida* means pale; and *trifoliata* means three-leafed.

Narrowleaf hoptree is widely distributed through the western two-thirds of New Mexico, northeastern Arizona, southern Colorado, Texas, and California. It might better be called a shrub in our area. The small trees are seldom over 6 feet tall and a few inches in diameter. The plant is readily identified by the compound leaves, usually with 3 leaflets, and by papery winged, hoplike fruits, consisting of 2 or 3 seeds surrounded by a light tan, papery wing about ½ to 5/8 inch in diameter, resembling elm fruits, only larger. The plant is not sufficiently common to be of much value to wildlife, although deer and Barbary sheep are known to eat the leaves. It appeared only in the deer food-habits study of the Guadalupe Mountains. The sapwood is pale straw colored and the heart is light brown, all with a very intricate ray pattern and iridescent. A synonym for this species is *P. baldwini*.

Pale hoptree has much the same description as narrowleaf but the leaves are smaller. It has a narrower range than narrowleaf. It occurs in the mountains of southern New Mexico, central and northern Arizona, and southwestern Texas. It is common around the Grand Canyon. It occurs at a somewhat lower elevation in the canyons and on the mesas than does narrowleaf hoptree.

A third species, *Ptelea trifoliata*, is common east of our area and has been listed as occurring in Carlsbad Caverns National Park.

Narrowleaf hoptree

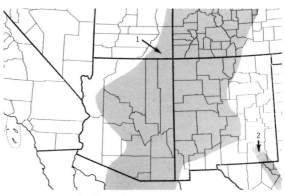

1. Narrowleaf hoptree
2. Common hoptree

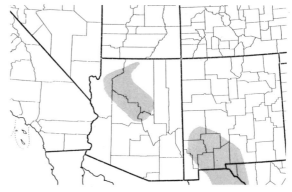

Pale hoptree

SAPODILLA FAMILY
(Sapotaceae)

Gum bumelia or chitamwood—*Bumelia lanuginosa* var. *rigida*
"Mulce"

    Bumelia is the classical name of the European ash; *lanuginosa* refers to the wooly hairs on the leaves; *rigida* refers to the rigid or stiff branches, which are somewhat thorny.

    Gum bumelia is found in Texas, in the extreme southwest corner of New Mexico, and in the southeastern corner of Arizona. It is not common but occurs along washes or on rocky hillsides. In Hidalgo County, New Mexico, it is found in several places along Animas wash as large clumps of small trees. The clumps are several hundred feet long and about 50 feet wide, with trees to 20 feet tall. In other places it occurs in small, scattered clumps. The trunks are generally only 4 to 6 inches in diameter, or smaller. The large clumps are heavily used by livestock seeking protection. Individual plants may be grazed so heavily they become hedged.

    The leaves are so dark green as to give the clumps a black appearance. The leaves are 1 to 1½ inches long, slender, and crowded at the nodes, which are swollen. The whitish, fragrant flowers appear in June and the ripe seeds are found in the fall. The fruits look like small olives, about ½ inch long, nearly black and one-seeded. The bark is fissured and somewhat scaly. The wood looks similar to ash wood. The sapwood is straw-colored and the heart is light golden color with attractive grain pattern. It is moderately hard and heavy and works easily.

Gum bumelia

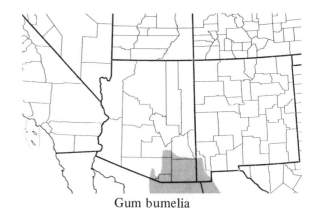

Gum bumelia

Gum bumelia

SAXIFRAGE FAMILY
(Saxifragaceae)

Cliff fendlerbush—*Fendlera rupicola*
Utah fendlerella—*Fendlerella utahensis*

Fendlera honors August Fendler, a German botanist who explored in New Mexico, and *rupicola* means "lover of rocks."

Cliff fendlerbush is certainly a "lover of rocks." As its name implies, it is found on dry hillsides, and is wide-spread through the mountain foothills and canyons of our area. The shrub grows to 6 feet tall and is normally slender, but because of heavy browsing it is usually shorter and badly hedged. The leaves are slender and small, with margins rolled under, and the many very small seeds are borne in pea-sized capsules. The white flowers have 4 petals and 8 stamens and are about 1" across. The wood, when a piece big enough to use can be found, has light straw-colored sapwood and light-brown heartwood. It shows so little grain that the color pattern resembles flown porcelain, giving it an appearance quite unique among woods. The plant resembles mockorange very closely, except that mockorange has numerous stamens.

Another very closely related shrub of this same family is *Fendlerella utahensis*, Utah fendlerella. It occurs in Utah and is said to occur in New Mexico and Arizona. The shrub is small and has small clusters of very small white flowers and later seed capsules about 1/8 inch in diameter.

Cliff fendlerbush is very valuable to browsing animals and is heavily utilized. Fendlerella is less desirable.

SAXIFRAGE FAMILY
(Saxifragaceae)

Cliff jamesia—*Jamesia americana*

Jamesia honors Edwin James, botanist for the Long expedition to the Rocky Mountains. America is the home range of the only species.

Cliff jamesia occurs in the higher mountains of our whole area and on northward as a shrub up to about 6 feet tall. It is another of the shrubs that is often found to be so

Cliff fendlerbush

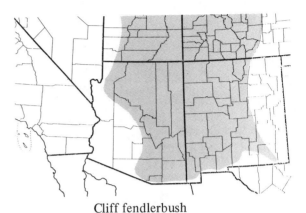

Cliff fendlerbush

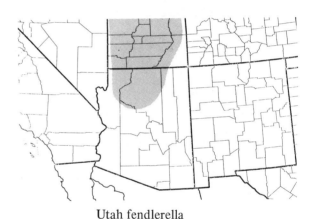

Utah fendlerella

Cliff jamesia

badly hedged as to mask its growth form. In the spring and summer, the small white flowers are borne in clusters at the ends of the branches and are quite showy. The small capsules are filled with numerous seeds. The simple, opposite leaves are oval, with prominent veins, and up to 2 inches long, bright green in color. The bark of the long, slender twigs flakes off in long, narrow strips. It is found in the ponderosa pine and up into higher zones, where it is heavily utilized by deer and elk.

Cliff jamesia

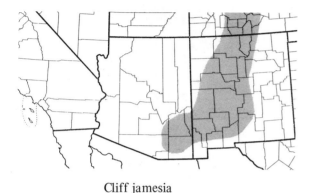

Cliff jamesia

SAXIFRAGE FAMILY
(Saxifragaceae)

Mockorange—*Philadelphus microphyllus*

The generic name is said to honor Ptolemy Philadelphus, ancient Egyptian king, and the specific name refers to the small leaves. This plant occurs widely spread through our area and westward in about the same habitat as cliff fendlerbush: dry hillsides and canyon walls in the foothills and into the mountains to about 8,000 feet. Its flower is also 4-petalled, white, about 1 inch across, but with numerous stamens. The leaves may be a little broader and more lance-shaped than those of cliff fendlerbush. That is, they are opposite, entire, and about 1 inch long, edges not rolled under. The plant has a somewhat spreading growth habit with slender and almost vinelike branches. The seed capsules are pea-sized, leathery, and filled with numerous seeds. This shrub is of minor importance to game.

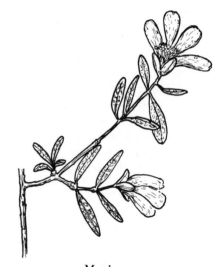

Mockorange

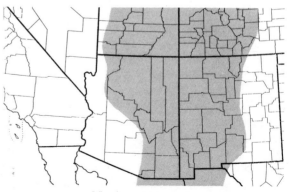

Mockorange

138

Mockorange

SAXIFRAGE FAMILY
(Saxifragaceae)

Black currant—*Ribes americanum*
Golden currant—*Ribes aureum*
Wax currant—*Ribes cereum*
Colorado currant—*Ribes coloradense*
Squaw currant—*Ribes inebrians*
Whitestem gooseberry—*Ribes inerme*
Trumpet gooseberry—*Ribes leptanthum*
Mescalero currant—*Ribes mescalerium*
Gooseberry currant—*Ribes montigenum*
Orange gooseberry—*Ribes pinetorum*
Sticky currant—*R. viscosissimum*
Rothrock currant—*Ribes wolfii*

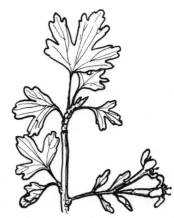

Black current

Ribs is a Danish word for red currant
and from it comes *ribes. Aureum* refers to
gold, *cereum* to wax; *inerme* means unarmed
(not wholly true in this species); *leptanthum*
means thin-flowered; *mescalerium* refers to
use by the Mescalero Indians; *montigeum*
refers to mountain habitat; *pinetorum* refers
to pineland habitat; *viscosissimum* refers to
stickiness; *wolfii* honors a man.

Various authors disagree on which
species of *Ribes* occur in our area, but the
above listed ones have been reported from
one or more of the national parks and monuments or national forests of our region. To
identify each in the field would take a detailed
botanical description beyond the scope of
this publication.

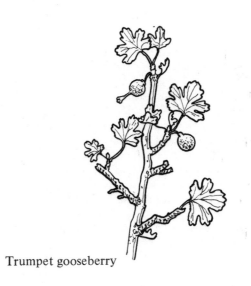

Trumpet gooseberry

139

These are generally low shrubs. Some species grow to about 6 feet tall in good locations. They are generally found in dense clumps on hillsides or in the river valleys. They occur from the plains, through the foothills and into the higher mountains. Some of the currants are virtually without spines and some of the gooseberries are so spiny that it is hard to gather the fruit. Both the currants and the gooseberries have berries large enough to warrant gathering. The American currant is black when ripe and makes delicious jelly. The golden currants are yellow and make a fine sauce. They are valuable for wildlife food and cover.

Since one species or another is found in every mountain range, distribution maps are largely meaningless.

Wax current

SOAPBERRY FAMILY
(Sapindaceae)

Mexican buckeye—*Ungnadia speciosa*

Ungnadia honors Baron Ungnad and *speciosa* means showy. Mexican buckeye is a small shrub to small tree of western Texas, south-central New Mexico and south into Mexico. It is not known from Arizona. I have found it in the Organ Mountains east of Las Cruces, where it grows as a small shrub among the rocks, and in the same type of habitat in the Guadalupe Mountains west of Carlsbad, New Mexico.

The fragrant rose-colored flowers occur in spring and are about 1 inch across. The leaves are compound with 5 to 7 leaflets to a stem, 3 to 5 inches long, and serrated along the margins. The seed capsules are 2 inches across, 3-celled but usually with one seed. They are borne on short stalks. The pods are brown and leathery and do not generally open wide enough to release the shiny black seed.

The dark gray bark of small stems would be smooth except that it is covered with very small warts. The wood is hard, heavy, and dense and very light yellow in color.

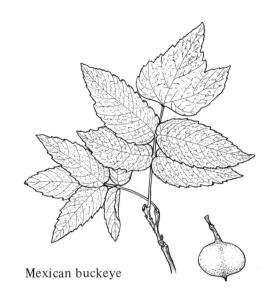

Mexican buckeye

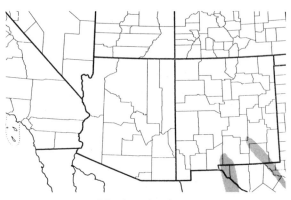

Mexican buckeye

SOAPBERRY FAMILY
(Sapindaceae)

Western soapberry—*Sapindus drummondii*
"Jaboncillo, Palo blanco"

In the scientific name, *Sapindus* is made up of the Latin word *sapo*, meaning soap, and *indicus*, the Latin for India; thus, soap of India. *Drummondii* honors Thomas Drummond, botanist. The tree is sometimes referred to as *S. saponaria* var. *drummondii*.

This is another small tree, seldom over 25 feet tall and several inches in diameter. It occurs in clumps in eastern and southern New Mexico and in southeastern and central Arizona, northwest below the Mogollon Rim to southern Coconino and Yavapai counties. The tree is not as confined to the desert washes as is desertwillow. It may be found in the dry foothills of the Burro Mountains southwest of Silver City, New Mexico, or out on the high plains of eastern New Mexico, where it is referred to locally as china-berry tree, a name that should be reserved for an entirely different tree, *Melia azedarach*, an import from southwest Asia.

This tree has been used rather extensively as an ornamental. The leaves are compound, 5 to 8 inches long with 13 to 19 leaflets. The flowers are borne in May to August in large clusters 6 to 9 inches long. The seeds are borne singly in yellow, translucent balls about ½ inch in diameter. The fruits contain an alkaloid, saponin, which is highly poisonous. The wood is heavy and medium hard, and open-grained. It finishes nicely. The color is light lemon yellow in sapwood and yellow to tan in the heart, flecked with tan. It has no commercial importance. The trees may be of some value to desert birds for nesting sites.

Western soapberry

Western soapberry

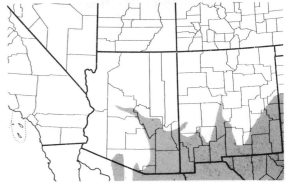

Western soapberry

141

SOAPBERRY FAMILY
(Sapindaceae)

Hop bush—*Dodonaea viscosa*
"Chapuliztle"

Hop bush occurs in our area in Arizona
from Verde River southward in scattered
localities and southeastward in Mexico. It
grows in the upper desert and grassland to
4,000 feet. It is a shrub or small tree up to
9 feet tall. The fruit bears 3 papery wings
that make it hoplike in appearance, somewhat
like hop tree. The seeds of this bush were
used in Hawaii in the preparation of a potion
to stun fish so that they could be more easily
captured. The narrow leaves are simple. The
flowers are small and yellowish in color.

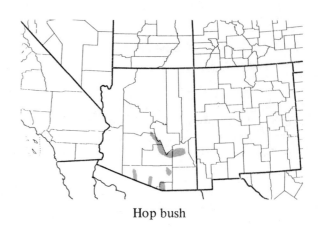
Hop bush

STAFF-TREE FAMILY
(Celastraceae)

Spiny grease-bush—*Forsellesia spinescens*

Forsellesia honors J.H. Forselles, a
Swedish botanical writer; *spinescens* refers to
the weakly spiny character of the plant.
Spiny grease-bush occurs in western
Texas, southern New Mexico, and westward
into California. It grows as a small shrub
about 3 feet high. The plant is intricately
branched and has weak spines. The stems are
green, the leaves are simple, alternate, and
very tiny. The small flowers occur singly in
the axils of the leaves along the upper end
of the branches. The tiny dark brown seeds
are shiny and minutely beaked. The plant
grows on dry, rocky limestone hills in the
lower mountains, and serves as feed for
mule deer and domestic stock.

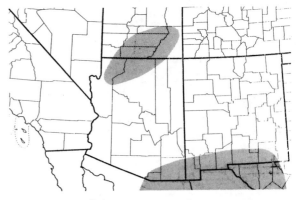
Spiny grease-wood

STAFF-TREE FAMILY
(Celastraceae)

Myrtle-boxleaf—*Pachystima myrsinites*

Pachys means thick and refers to the thickened stigma, while the species name refers to the resemblance to the genus *Myrsine.*

Myrtle-boxleaf occurs in the high mountains of New Mexico, west to California, and north to Canada. It is generally found from the ponderosa pine zone upward to nearly timberline as a low or prostrate shrub rarely over 3 feet in height. The leaves are simple, opposite, small, smooth or serrate toward the tip, and somewhat curled at the edges, with a smooth surface. The flowers, in small clusters at the leaf axils, are very small. The tiny seed capsule contains one or two seeds. The plant serves as ground cover in the high mountain forest and as cover for forest-dwelling wildlife.

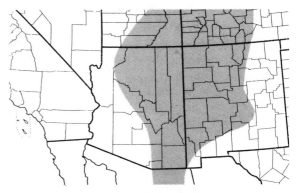

Myrtle-boxleaf

STAFF-TREE FAMILY
(Celastraceae)

Crucifixion-thorn
"Corona de Cristo"
Canotia holacantha

The name *holacantha* is derived from Greek words that literally mean wholly thorn, and this shrub is made up almost wholly of thorns.

Canotia might be confused with all-thorn, *Koeberlinia spinosa.* However, *Canotia* becomes a larger tree, the berries are much larger, and the thorns are long and forked at acute angles.

Canotia occurs in southeastern California, far south in Utah and in Arizona in the Mohave Desert and in the lower edge of the chaparral and upper part of the Sonoran desert. I saw a good specimen near Mayer, Arizona, north of Phoenix. The tree becomes nearly 20 feet tall and about 1 foot in diameter, with several heavy branches made up of the long, green thorns arranged like the straws of a broom. The thorns are yellowish-green and appear to be covered with faint parallel lines. The fruits are about 3/8 inch in diameter and ½ inch long with a sharp point, reddish in color. The fruits

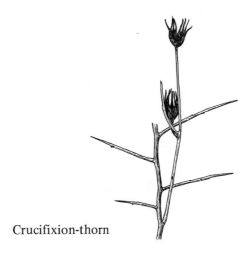

Crucifixion-thorn

Crucifixion-thorn

143

hang on until they are weathered and nearly black, at which time the point has frayed or partially opened. The wood is light brown in color with straw-colored sapwood streaked with pink. The plant has little value except as cover for nesting birds.

It is interesting to note that Benson and Darrow included *Canotia* in the *Koeberliniaceae* family, while Little and Kearney and Peebles place it in the *Celastraceae* family.

Crucifixion-thorn

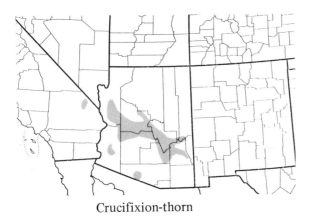

Crucifixion-thorn

SUMAC FAMILY
(Anacardiaceae)

Poison ivy—*Toxicodendron radicans*
Western poison ivy—*T. rydbergia*

Toxicodendron derives its meaning from the root *toxicon*, meaning poison, and *dendron*, meaning tree. *Radicans* refers to the climbing habit of the eastern form. *Rydbergia* honors P. A. Rydberg, early Colorado botanist. The naming of poison ivy is confusing, as some authors consider western poison ivy to be merely a non-climbing form of *T. radicans*, the poison ivy of the East. Other writers give it the generic name of *Rhus.* It is hardly a large enough shrub to include in this publication, but is included because of its poisonous nature. Anyone looking for shrubs should be aware of poison ivy and avoid it, as the skin irritation caused by contact with the plant is troublesome to cure. The plant is recognized by the 3 leaflets of the compound leaf. It is seldom more than 1 foot tall in our area. The leaves, arranged alternately, turn bright red in fall. Bunches of white berries are borne in the leaf axils. The leaves are long-stalked and attached to a short, woody stem. The plant is widespread through the plains, foothills, and into the ponderosa pine zone. No distribution map is needed.

SUMAC FAMILY
(*Anacardiaceae*)

Skunkbush or squawbush–*Rhus trilobata*
"Agrillo, Lemita"
Littleleaf sumac–*Rhus microphylla*
"Agritos"
Mearns' sumac–*Rhus choriophylla*
Kearney sumac–*Rhus kearneyi*
Sugar sumac–*Rhus ovata*
Smooth sumac–*Rhus glabra*
Prairie flame-leaf sumac–*Rhus copallina* var.
        lanceolata
Evergreen sumac–*Rhus virens* or *sempervirens*
        "Zumaque"
Utah squawbush–*Rhus utahensis*

In this treatment of the Anacardiaceae family, I have chosen to follow the lead of the writers that separate Rhus and Toxicodendron. *Rhus* is the ancient Latin word. The meanings of the specific names are as follows:

Trilobata–3-lobed, referring to the shape of
        the leaf
Microphylla–literally, small-leafed
Choriophylla–many-leafed
Kearneyi–honors Thomas H. Kearney
Ovata–refers to the ovate shape of the leaves
Glabra–smooth
Copallina–copal gum; *lanceolata* refers to the
        lance shape of the leaves
Virens–green
Utahensis–named for the State

Skunkbush earns its name because of the evil smell of the crushed leaves. In spite of this, it is readily taken by deer. In fact, skunkbush is the shrub that has appeared more more consistently than any other in deer food studies and other studies of the food of antelope, Barbary sheep, elk, and desert bighorns in New Mexico. It also was a preferred food in the food preference trials run at Los Alamos. This steady pruning by browsing animals may account in part for the rounded, compact form of many of the bushes. The plant is easily recognized by the abundant dark red fruit borne in small clusters, by the trifoliate leaves, and by the evil smell. The stems are slender. The thin sapwood is white and the heartwood is pinkish red. There is a narrow band of gray-green wood between the sap and the heartwood, a characteristic common to many woods of this genus. The plant is of considerable value in conservation plantings and is often referred to as squawbush or quailbush. The form of the bush varies somewhat from place to place. On Mt. Taylor, I found bushes with trunks 2 or more inches in diameter that grew, in part, along the ground in a long and crooked shape.

Skunkbush
(Occurs through area)

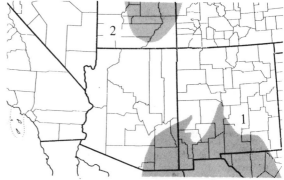

1. Littleleaf sumac
2. Utah squawbush

Mearns' sumac

145

In the Chiricahua Mountains it was noticed that the crown of the bush was much more open and the stems taller than is common. This species is very widely distributed through West Texas, New Mexico, Arizona to California. It is very common over much of its range.

Littleleaf sumac is not as widespread in our region. It follows the location of the Lower Sonoran Zone and reaches its best development in the southern part of our area and on into Mexico. A shrub of the desert washes and valleys, it is easily distinguished by its rounded shape, dark green color, and large size of the bushes, up to 10 feet tall in our area. The reddish orange fruit is hairy, the small leaves are odd-pinnately compound with 5 to 9 very small leaflets. The sapwood is white and the heart is dark gray to black. A striking black band separates the heartwood from the sapwood. The wood is difficult to saw because of the long, tough fibers. It is moderately lightweight and soft. The shrub has little wildlife value but may be browsed lightly by deer at times.

Mearns' sumac, or New Mexico evergreen sumac as it is sometimes called, is a very beautiful shrub with shiny, bright green compound leaves of generally 5 leaflets. The distribution is even more restricted than that of littleleaf sumac. It can be found in the mountains of extreme southwest New Mexico, southern Arizona and south into Mexico.

Kearney sumac is reported from one mountain range in southwestern Arizona, the Tinajas Altas Mountains in southern Yuma County. It is a large evergreen shrub with simple leaves. The fruit is reddish and hairy, characteristic of the genus.

Sugar sumac, also called sugar bush in southern California, is a small, compact, rounded shrub generally less than 10 feet tall. The simple, ovate, evergreen leaves are about 1½ to 3 inches long, bright green, shiny, and appearing partly folded along the midrib. The fruit is reddish and hairy with a sweet taste. The distribution in our area is limited to the Arizona chaparral type found in central Arizona and also in a similar type in southern California. The wood is less stringy than littleleaf or skunkbush and light brown in color. I saw one specimen in the mountains south of Prescott that was 10 feet tall and with a well-developed trunk 1 foot in diameter.

Smooth sumac occurs in southeastern New Mexico and east. It is a thicket former, generally a shrub but treelike in favorable sites. It is very similar to the staghorn sumac used as an ornamental. The compound leaves may have as many as 31 leaflets. The white flowers occur in a terminal cluster. The seeds are also in a dense cluster, are covered with short velvety red hairs and

Sugar sumac

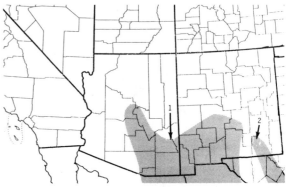

1. Mearns' sumac
2. Prairie flame-leaf sumac

Prairie flame-leaf sumac

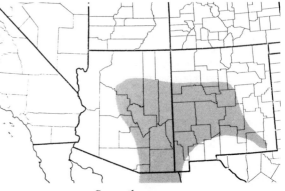

Smooth sumac

are taken by various species of birds. The wood is orange and soft. A synonym for this sumac is *R. cismontana*.

Prairie flame-leaf sumac is limited in our area to southeastern New Mexico but occurs eastward into Texas and south into Mexico. It is distinguished by the brilliance of leaf coloring in the fall and by the showy red cluster of fruits at the ends of the branches. Otherwise, it is very similar to smooth sumac.

Evergreen sumac is another of the sumacs which occurs only in southeastern New New Mexico in our area, and in Texas and Mexico. It forms rounded clumps similar to skunkbush. The compound leaves have up to 9 leaflets, short, broad, and darker green than in Mearns' sumac. The flowers, and later the fruits, occur as small clusters at the axils of the leaves. The small fruits are covered with short red hairs.

Utah squawbush or sumac occurs in Utah and Arizona and possibly west into California. It is different from the other sumacs in that it has simple, undivided leaves, rounded or kidney-shaped. It occurs in the sagebrush country and is of little or no value.

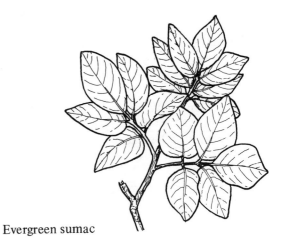

Evergreen sumac

Evergreen sumac

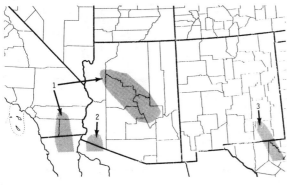

1. Sugar sumac
2. Kearney sumac
3. Evergreen sumac

SYCAMORE FAMILY
(Platanaceae)

Arizona sycamore—*Platanus wrightii*
"Alamo, Alamo blanco"

Platanus is the classical name for plane tree, as European sycamore is known. The specific name honors Thomas Wright.

This tree occurs along the stream banks and flood plains in southwestern New Mexico and southeastern Arizona to the central part. Many small but beautiful stands of this tree may be seen in the Gila and Coronado National Forests, in Guadalupe Canyon in extreme southwest New Mexico, and along Rucker Creek as it extends out of the west side of the Chiricahua Mountains of Arizona. The tree grows to a very large size, 80 feet tall and 4 feet in diameter in good sites, or, reportedly, much larger on Beaver Creek in Arizona. The seed occurs in pendant balls about 1 inch in diameter, hanging on stalks 6 to 8 inches long. The most useful identifying characteristic of the tree is the light green color of the bark on the branches, which grades from dark gray to white where the old bark flakes off. The wood is hard and heavy, with the very strong ray pattern characteristic of sycamore. The wood is beautiful light pink in color, but care must be taken in harvesting it, as it spoils rather quickly in the log. A small amount could be used in making speciality products, but it serves a better purpose left unharvested for its esthetic value.

Along protected streams like Animas on the east side of the Black Range and Rucker in Arizona, sycamore may be found growing for many miles from the mouth of the canyon. As an added attraction, the leaves color beautifully in the fall as they turn yellow and russet.

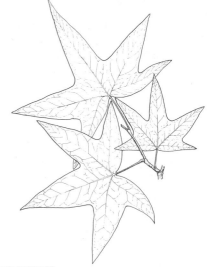

Arizona sycamore

Arizona sycamore

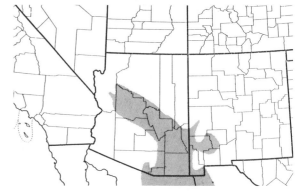

Arizona sycamore

148

TAMARISK FAMILY
(Tamaricaceae)

French tamarisk—*Tamarix gallica*
Five-stamen tamarisk—*T. pentandra*
Athel tamarisk—*T. aphylla*

Tamarisk is another of the trees that has been introduced from a foreign land and become naturalized in our region. The generic name is of obscure origin. *Gallica* refers to a Gallic tribe, *pentandra* refers to the 5 stamens in the flower, and *aphylla* literally means without leaves. There is considerable confusion about the naming of the tamarisk or saltcedar as it is also called. It is now generally considered that the commonly found tamarisk in the river valleys of the West is *Tamarix pentandra*. French tamarisk has limited distribution.

Five-stamen tamarisk is a large shrub or small tree seldom exceeding 25 feet in height. Trees planted in yards occasionally grow quite large. The prize example is a tree in Albuquerque that measures 7' 3" in circumference and 44' tall with a crown spread of 45'. Five-stamen tamarisk was introduced from Asia Minor as an ornamental and for a time was distributed for use in windbreak plantings. However, it escaped from cultivation and now covers hundreds of thousands of acres in the river valleys of the West. It extends up the river valleys to about 7,000 feet elevation. It produces very thick stands.

The leaves are scalelike along a wiry stem. The minute pink flowers cover the flower stems in season, making this a showy tree and explaining its value as an ornamental. The very small seeds are borne in large quantities and germinate readily if they fall on bare, wet soil such as exposed mud flats. Seed sometimes germinates under much less favorable circumstances.

The wood is a very pretty dark brown mixed with streaks of pink, but the trees are too small and crooked for commercial utilization. The tree has become useful for cover. No distribution map is needed, as the tree occupies valley bottoms throughout our area to about 7,000 feet.

Athel tamarisk has been used as an ornamental in southern New Mexico and Arizona. It is a much more handsome tree than 5-stamen tamarisk and reminds the viewer of Casuarina. Large specimens may be seen in the area of Superior, Arizona and other places. The stems with their minute leaves are long and drooping and bright green. The flowers are similar to 5-stamen tamarisk. Trees were seen that were 2 feet in diameter and 40 feet tall.

Tamarisk

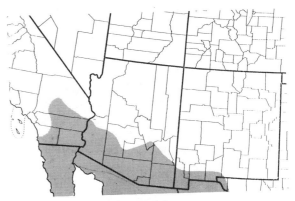

Athel tamarisk

149

TRUMPET-CREEPER FAMILY
(Bignoniaceae)

Desertwillow—*Chilopsis linearis*
"Mimbre"

The desertwillow is not a willow at all, but belongs to the same family as the catalpa. In the scientific name *Chilopsis* refers to the lip-like appearance of the corolla, and *linearis* signifies long and slender, as are the seed pod and leaves. The flowers may occur from April to August and are quite showy. They grade from white to pink and purple, are 1 to 1¼ inches long and tubular. The leaves are only about 3/8 inch wide and up to 6 inches long, and the seed capsules are ¼ inch in diameter and 4 to 8 inches long. The small, poorly formed trees or large shrubs grow to a height of about 25 feet in the dry washes and river valleys of New Mexico from Roswell south and from just north of Albuquerque south into Mexico. In Arizona, desertwillow occurs from the southeastern corner, across the central portion to the far northwestern corner and over into southern Nevada and southwestern Utah.

The wood is soft, medium weight, and uniform medium brown in color, intricately flecked with minute rays. It has no commercial value. The trees are heavily browsed by livestock in some areas and furnish cover and nesting sites for desert birds.

TRUMPET-CREEPER FAMILY
(Bignoniaceae)

Yellow trumpet—*Tecoma stans*
"Tornadora"

Tecoma is from an Indian word meaning pot-tree, and *stans* refers to the upright growth of the shrub. The yellow trumpet of our area is probably variety *angustata*. It occurs widely through western and southern Texas, southern New Mexico, Arizona, and south into Mexico.

The yellow, trumpet-shaped flowers are similar in shape to the flowers of the more common desertwillow of the same family. The plant is usually a shrub but may be treelike. The flat seeds are less than ¼ inch long, winged, and borne in a long slender, beanlike pod up to 6 inches long. The leaves are pinnately compound with 7 to 9 or more leaflets, pointed at base and tip. The wood is said to have been used by Indians in making bows.

Desertwillow

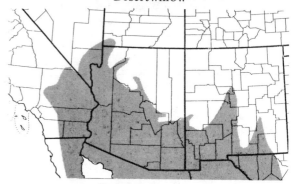
Desertwillow

Yellow trumpet

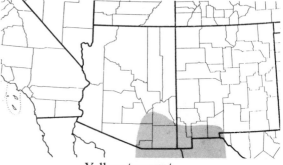
Yellow trumpet

150

VERBENA FAMILY
(Verbenaceae)

High-mass—*Aloysia wrightii*

A common synonym for the scientific name is *Lippia wrightii*. *Aloysia* is in honor of Maria Louisa, wife of Charles IV of Spain, and *wrightii* honors Charles Wright, American botanist.

High-mass occurs in western Texas, New Mexico, Arizona, and south into Mexico, where it is often common up to 6,000 feet elevation on dry hillsides. It grows as a shrub, generally about 2 feet tall but up to 6 feet. The small, rounded leaves are deciduous, opposite, slightly serrate, and hairy. The flowers are borne on paired spikes at or near the ends of the stems. They are tiny and white. The fruits consist of two small, thin-walled segments, each containing a small nutlet. The stems are brittle and 4-angled with fibrous bark. They are very slender.

The plant is considered to be a good honey producer and is browsed by cattle.

WALNUT FAMILY
(Juglandaceae)

Little walnut—*Juglans microcarpa*
"Nogal"

The generic name is a contraction of Latin *Jovis glans*, acorn of Jupiter. *Microcarpa* means little nut, thus little walnut.

Little walnut occurs along the east slopes of the Guadalupe and Capitan Mountains in southeast New Mexico to the Pecos River. It occurs locally along the water courses that extend out from the foothills to the plains. The nuts are readily taken by squirrels and rodents, but the trees are otherwise important only as cover.

The leaves are pinnately compound with 13 to 23 leaflets. The leaflets are narrow and long and finely toothed. The nuts are the smallest of all walnuts, seldom more than ½ inch in diameter. The hard, brown, porous wood resembles black and Arizona walnut in color and texture. It also has poorly cemented annual rings and literally comes apart when being worked. This quality, plus the small size of the trees, eliminates any practical use for the wood. The nuts are utilized by squirrels but otherwise the tree has little value for wildlife. One deer, killed in the desert adjacent to the Guadalupe Mountains, had filled its stomach with leaves and twigs.

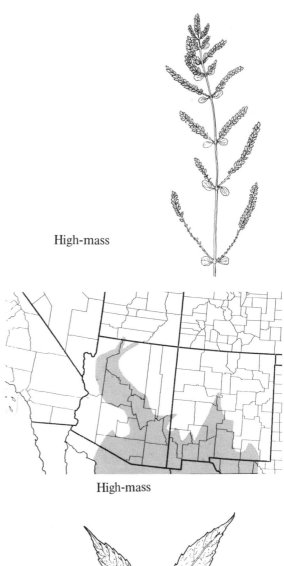

High-mass

High-mass

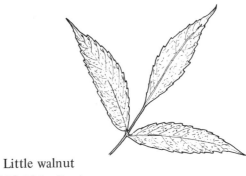

Little walnut
(13-23 leaflets)

Little walnut

151

WALNUT FAMILY
(Juglandaceae)

Arizona walnut–*Juglans major*
"Nogal silvestre"

Major means large, but the nuts of this walnut are intermediate in size between the little walnut of New Mexico and common black walnuts. The Arizona walnut or nogal occurs in the southwest quarter of New Mexico from the Capitan Mountains south and west. In Arizona it occurs in the southeast and central mountains and locally in Havasu Canyon. It extends south into Mexico.

It grows in the canyon bottoms and along creeks in the mountains in the ponderosa pine zone and along washes in the foothills. It often occurs in somewhat drier sites than the closely associated Arizona sycamores, Arizona alder, velvet ash, Fremont cottonwood, and willows. It generally grows in scattered stands as a small, branched tree. In at least one location on Apache Creek in New Mexico it grows to 80 feet or more in height and 3 feet in diameter.

The leaves are pinnately compound, with 9 to 13 or more leaflets to the stem. The nuts are smaller than the well-known black walnuts, but are edible if one has the patience to shuck and shell them. The hard, brown, porous wood resembles black walnut, but is more brash and tends to separate at the growth rings. The well-seasoned wood works nicely and might be used commercially except for its scattered occurrence. The nuts are readily taken by squirrels and rodents, but the trees are otherwise important only as cover.

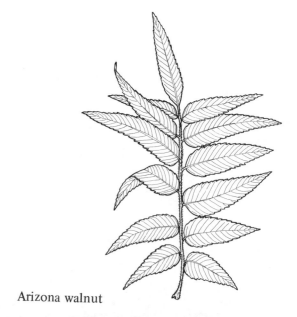
Arizona walnut

Arizona walnut

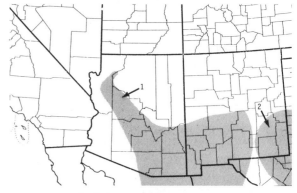
1. Arizona walnut
2. Little walnut

152

WILLOW FAMILY
(Salicaceae)

Sargent's or plains cottonwood—*Populus sargentii*

The cottonwoods are all of the genus *Populus*. This may have been derived from *arbor populi*, a Roman expression meaning people's tree. *Sargentii* honors an early botanist and dendrologist.

All cottonwoods, in their native habitat, are limited to watercourses. Sargent's cottonwood is limited to the extreme northeast corner of New Mexico and on north through Colorado and into Kansas. The same botanical description quite generally fits Sargent's, Rio Grande, and Gila cottonwood. All have a broad, triangular leaf, 2 or more inches long and 2½ to 3 inches wide; long-stemmed; pointed at apex and with margin toothed. The seeds are borne in capsules attached to a long stalk and bearing many cottony seeds that give the tree its name. The bark is rough and deep-furrowed on old trunks, but smooth and whitish green in the upper branches. The trees are large, growing to 100 feet tall and 4 or more feet in diameter with wide-spreading crowns.

The cottonwoods all furnish choice food and dam-building materials for beaver, browse for elk and deer, buds and cambium for squirrels, and cover for all wildlife that frequent the streams and the adjacent wooded bosques along the streams.

The wood is lightweight, soft, tough, and long-fibered. The wood of plains cottonwoods is the most nearly white of all. The wood is used for fuel and for very short-lived posts and corral poles and can be used as lumber in rough construction, if properly cured. Due to the long fibers, it is also good for veneer core stock and pulpwood.

WILLOW FAMILY
(Salicaceae)

Rio Grande cottonwood—*Populus wislizeni* "Alamo" or "Guerigo"

This cottonwood was also named in honor of an early botanist. Some botanists consider it to be a variety of *Populus fremontii*. In this case they use the common name as Fremont cottonwood, making it difficult to keep in mind which cottonwood is being considered. In this publication, it is considered to be a separate species, following Little.

This cottonwood fits the same general description as mentioned under Sargent's

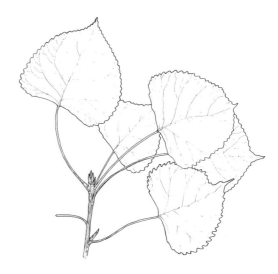

Sargent's cottonwood

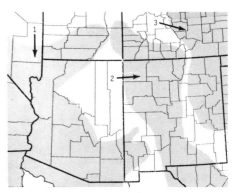

1. Fremont cottonwood
2. Rio Grande cottonwood
3. Sargent's cottonwood

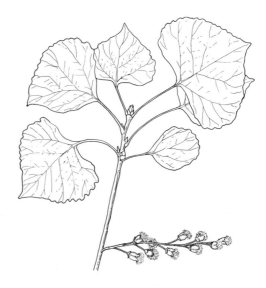

Rio Grande cottonwood

153

cottonwood. However, the stalks of the seed capsules are longer than the seed capsules. It is seldom that the viewer will have this characteristic to help him.

The tree occurs along the Rio Grande from Mexico across New Mexico to southern Colorado and in the San Juan basin in northwest New Mexico and southwest Colorado. The heartwood of this tree is deeper brown than that of Fremont cottonwood but the sapwood is white. It has the same uses and fills the same ecological niche in its range as do Fremont and Sargent's cottonwood.

WILLOW FAMILY
(Salicaceae)

Fremont or Gila cottonwood–*Populus fremontii*
"Alamo"

This cottonwood was named in honor of John C. Fremont, early explorer of the West. It fits the same general description as that given for Sargent's cottonwood. There are minor differences in the flowers and in other technical details and, in general, the leaves of Fremont cottonwood are somewhat smaller than those of Sargent's. This is a relative matter, as one may find very large leaves on young sprouts and smaller leaves on old growth of either species. Since Fremont cottonwood occurs in southwestern New Mexico and on west across Arizona to California, the ranges of the two do not overlap and a person may best distinguish them geographically.

Some botanists consider Rio Grande cottonwood to be a variety of Fremont cottonwood. This makes it hard to distinguish geographically between these two similar species. Rio Grande cottonwood will be discussed as *Populus wislizeni* in this publication.

The heartwood of Fremont cottonwood is streaked with light brown but the sapwood is white. Fremont cottonwood has the same uses as Sargent's and fills a very similar ecological niche where it is found.

A very large old tree of this species may be seen growing in one of the animal pens of the Red Rock Wildlife Area of the New Mexico Department of Game and Fish in southwestern New Mexico. I measured this tree in 1971 and found it to be 27' 10" in circumference and 84' 7" tall, with a crown spread of 114'. It is truly a monarch of its kind, exceeded in size only by one growing near Patagonia, Arizona.

Rio Grande cottonwood

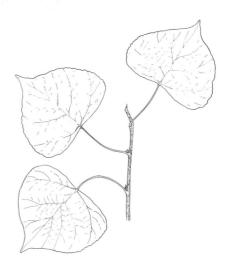

Fremont cottonwood

Fremont cottonwood

WILLOW FAMILY
(Salicaceae)

Narrowleaf cottonwood—*Populus angustifolia*

Angustifolia literally means narrowleaf. The tree is sometimes confused with willow because of the narrow leaf. However, the normal tree form of the narrowleaf cotton-wood is tall and slender. The bark of the upper trunk and branches is whitish, as is characteristic of the broad-leafed cotton-woods but not of the willows. The bark on the old growth is not as deeply furrowed as the broad-leafed cottonwoods. The heart-wood is streaked with light brown color much as is that of Fremont cottonwood.

Narrowleaf cottonwood grows along streams but generally at a higher altitudinal range than the broad-leafed species. It will be found as a streamside tree of the ponderosa pine zone above the broad-leafed forms and below aspen. It has the same uses as the other cottonwoods.

Narrowleaf cottonwood

Narrowleaf cottonwood

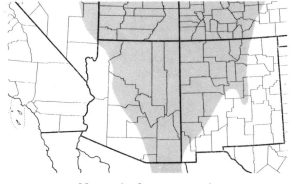

Narrowleaf cottonwood

WILLOW FAMILY
(Salicaceae)

Lanceleaf cottonwood—*Populua acuminata*

The specific name, *acuminata*, means tapering at the end. Elbert Little mentions that Ernest Rouleau considers this cotton-wood to be a cross between Sargent's and narrowleaf cottonwoods. I prefer to follow the authors who have given it true specific rank because it is hard to understand how it would be found in some of the places where it is known if it were a hybrid. It occurs in the upper part of the Cimarron Canyon in northern New Mexico, miles from the nearest known Sargent's cottonwood, and in Fort Bayard pasture in southern New Mexico, several hundred miles from Sargent's cotton-wood.

Lanceleaf cottonwood

155

The leaves of this cottonwood are intermediate in shape between the long narrow form of narrowleaf and the triangular form of the broad-leafed species. The other characteristics are very similar.

All cottonwoods are troublesome to hay-fever sufferers because of the cotton that flies thickly in the early summer as the seeds ripen. Since the male flowers and female flowers are borne on separate trees, the problem can be controlled locally by planting only male trees and selectively cutting out the female trees. Many towns in the West have worked to do just this. The fact remains that, in its range, the cottonwood makes a very fine shade tree. It withstands more climatic variations than any of the trees that have been introduced from other areas for shade trees.

WILLOW FAMILY
(Salicaceae)

Aspen—*Populus tremuloides*
"Alamillo"

Aspen is widely distributed in the higher mountains of the western two-thirds of New Mexico and in eastern Arizona from the Chiricahua Mountains in the south, west through the center of the State to the Kaibab Plateau of the north. It extends on north across the mountain states and east across Canada and the northeastern United States. It is also called golden, trembling, or quaking aspen. *Populus* may be from *arbor populi*, Latin for people's tree. *Tremuloides*, the specific name, is derived from *tremula*, the species name of the European aspen and meaning trembling, plus *oides*, a suffix meaning resembling or similar to. Thus, our aspen resembles European aspen.

Aspen occurs in a wide band across the mountain ranges from the upper part of the Transition Zone, through the Canadian Zone to the lower part of the Hudsonian Zone.

It is a small- to medium-sized tree that grows about 50 feet high and seldom more than 20 inches in diameter, except on very good sites. Trees in many mature stands average no larger than poles. In a stand of aspen in the Pecos Wilderness, the largest tree was 11' 6" in circumference and 70' tall. Until it fell, it was the largest aspen recorded in the United States. Utah now claims the largest tree.

Aspens pioneer on burned areas and serve as a nurse crop to conifers that eventually replace them. This process is referred to by ecologists as succession. Theoretically, the mountains would eventually be covered with conifers if the process continued long enough without setbacks.

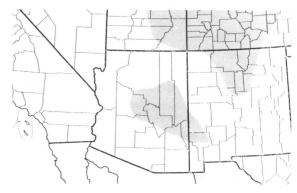

Lanceleaf cottonwood

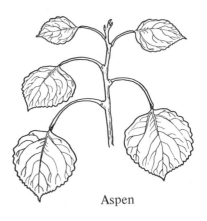

Aspen

Aspen

156

The broad leaves with pointed apex and serrated edges are rounded at the base and attached to the limbs with a flattened petiole or stem. This flattened stem allows the leaves to flutter or tremble in the faintest breeze. The small, inconspicuous flowers occur in early summer. The seed capsules burst open and release the cottony seeds in midsummer. The extreme lightness of the seed, easily wind-borne, probably accounts for the very wide-spread occurrence of this tree. The bark is almost white and smooth, characteristics that, unfortunately, make it attractive to people who like to carve on tree trunks. Aspen also spreads readily from suckers and root sprouts. This characteristic often accounts for the almost miraculous appearance of young stands following fires or other clearing operations, even though only a few old mature trees existed prior to the disturbance.

Aspen stands are preferred cover for deer and elk and contribute feed to these animals and also to squirrels and beaver. Deer feed on tender shoots and any leaves in reach and use the trees as rubbing posts when they are polishing their antlers. Recent research in Arizona shows that deer prefer mature leaves. Elk use the trees in the same way and, in addition, are able to break down saplings to reach the tender growth of the tree tops. Squirrels eat the cambium of the twigs and the buds. Beaver store logs in their ponds and then eat the bark in the winter. Aspens serve as cover for all wildlife of the associated forest. Beaver also use the wood widely in dam construction.

The sapwood is white and the heart is light brown, frequently with dark brown streaks, soft, lightweight, and tough. It cures out virtually taste- and odor-free and so is used for honeycomb dividers and food boxes. The light weight and toughness make it sought-after for plywood core stock and shipping pallets. The long fibers make it good for pulp used in making high-grade paper.

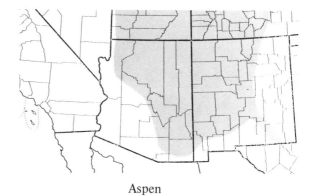

Aspen

WILLOW FAMILY
(Salicaceae)

Arroyo willow—*Salix lasiolepis*
(woolly-scaled)
Bebb willow—*S. bebbiana*
(honors Michael Bebb, American botanist)
Blue willow—*S. subcoerulea* (coerulea means blue and may refer to the bluish bloom on the stems)
Blue stem willow—*S. irrorata* (unwanted)
Bonpland willow—*S. bonplandiana* (honors Aimee Bonpland, French botanist)
Coyote willow—*S. exigua* (small or poor)
Dusky willow—*S. melanopsis* (dark or dusky twigs)
Goodding willow—*S. gooddingii* (honors Leslie Goodding, U.S.D.A. botanist)
Mountain or Scouler willow—*S. scouleriana* (honors John Scouler, Scotch naturalist)
Mountain willow—*S. monticola* (mountain dweller)
Pacific willow—*S. lasiandra* (refers to pubescent stamen)
Peachleaf willow—*S. amygdaloides* (similar to almond)
Peachleaf willow, Wrights—*S. amygdaloides* var. *wrightii* (honors Charles Wright)
Red willow—*S. laevigata* (smooth; refers to shiny, hairless leaves)
Rydberg willow—*S. pseudocordata* (literally, false heart-shape)
Sandbar willow—*S. interior* (refers to inland distribution)
Summit willow—*S. saximontana* (refers to mountainous, rocky habitat)
Whiplash willow—*S. caudata* var. *bryantiana* (caudata means with a tail; bryantiana honors Bryant)
Yellow willow—*S. lutea* (yellow)
Yewleaf willow—*S. taxifolia* (literally means yew-leafed)

The individual kinds of willows are hard to distinguish because of the leaves, twigs, and other characteristics do not vary enough between species to insure easy identification. It is often possible to decide which willow you have by considering shrub or tree size, location and, after narrowing down the possibilities, the more minute characteristics. The color of the wood can also serve as a valuable clue to identification.

Willows furnish shade and cover for all wildlife, food and dam material for beaver, browse for deer and elk. The leaves of willows are frequently browsed by grazing animals as high as the animals can reach. Shrub willows are frequently browsed back to near ground-line in winter, but grow back readily when the grazing pressure is removed.

Willows, like other stream-side trees, shade the water, helping to keep it cool for trout. As willows most frequently grow along the streams, they serve to protect the stream banks from erosion. They also furnish shade for animals and a poor grade of firewood for campers or picnickers.

The list I have given represents the most common willows of the area. Space does not permit sufficient detail for positive identification of all the species.

WILLOW FAMILY
(Salicaceae)

The following gives common names (1), distribution (2), characteristics (3), and uses (4) of the willows.

ARROYO ("Ahnejote"). (2) Mts. of SW New Mexico and eastern Ariz. (3) Shrub. Slender erect branches; twig yellow to brown; leaves narrow and long, margins smooth. Bark brown to gray. (4) Sapwood white, heart brown; too small to use.

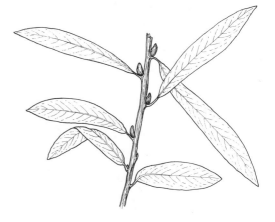

Arroyo willow

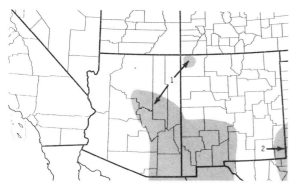

1. Arroyo willow
2. Sandbar willow

BEBB. (2) NE corner and mts. of northwest N.M. eastern and northern Ariz. and northward. (3) Large shrub to small tree, often in tight clumps. Small leaves with surface white to gray. (4) Sapwood white; heartwood gray-black;weak and small.

BLUE. (2) Aspen and spruce forest and meadows of high mountains, N.M., westward to Calif. and northward. (3) Small shrub to 9 ft. Leaves about 3" by ½". Twigs purplish to brown or black. (4) Not known. Small.

BLUE-STEM. (2) Along streams, eastern Colo., N.M. and Ariz, 5,500 to 7,500 ft. (3) Shrub to 12'. Reddish-brown stems very glaucous. Leaves to 4" by ½", lower surface white. (4) Not known. Small.

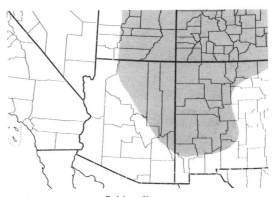

Bebb willow
(in high mountains)

Blue-stem willow

159

BONPLAND ("Sauz"). (2) Extreme SW corner of N.M.; SE and central Ariz. and southward. (3) Small tree to 50' tall. Slender twigs red to purple. Long, narrow, sharp-pointed leaves. Twigs first yellow, later brown. (4) Sapwood white; small heart light brown. Trunks to 20" diameter.

Bonpland willow

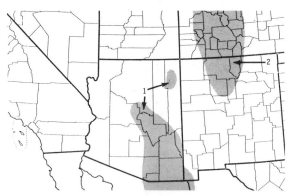

1. Bonpland willow
2. Mountain willow

COYOTE. (2) Common thicket-former on ditch banks, west 2/3 N.M. and over mts. of Ariz. and northward. (3) Small shrub to 12' or locally a small tree. Twigs yellow and silvery haired, leaves very narrow, 4" by ½". (4) Too small to use except for basket weaving.

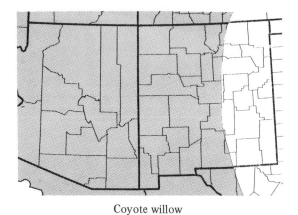

Coyote willow

Coyote willow

DUSKY. (2) Reported from monuments of SE Utah. (3) Tall shrub to 15'. Twigs brown or blackish, often lustrous. Leaves about 3" by ½"; dark green and smooth above, silky beneath. (4) Not known. Small.

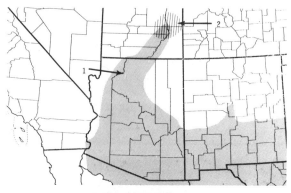

1. Goodding willow
2. Dusky willow

GOODDING ("Sauz"). (2) So. N.M. and up Rio Grande to Bernalillo and along streams, across So. Ariz. to Calif. (3) Med. tree to 50' by 2' to 3' dia. Twigs yellow. Leaves to 6" by 3/4", curved. Bark thick, rough, deeply furrowed. (4) White with very light tan streaks. Works well.

Goodding willow

MOUNTAIN OR SCOULER. (2) High mts. of No. 2/3 of N.M. 8,000 to 10,000 ft.; high mts. of Ariz., Grand Canyon and northward. (3) Large shrub to small tree, 4" in dia. Tight clumps with rounded crown. Leaves about 3" by 1", club-shaped. Bark thin. (4) Wood generally honey-yellow or tinged with red. Too small to use.

Scouler willow

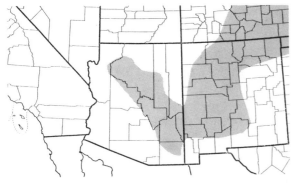

Scouler willow

Scouler willow

Map combined with Bonpland willow

MOUNTAIN. (2) Very high mts. No. N.M., Colo., Utah and northward. (3) Shrub to 18'. Leaves about 2" by 1"; tip and base narrowed. Twigs first yellowish, later reddish brown. (4) Not known.

PACIFIC. (2) 5,000 to 7,000 ft. west and north N.M.
Ariz. in White Mts. and Tonto Basin and northward.
(3) Small tree to 40' by 15". Lance-shaped leaves,
long pointed. Twigs bright yellow in spring. Green
scale at base each leaf. (4) Wide, white sapwood;
small heart grayish-black. Works well.

Pacific willow

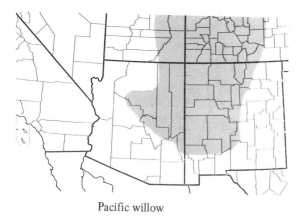

Pacific willow

PEACHLEAF. (2) Common No. N.M. and down river
to south border; rare in E Ariz., common northward.
(3) Small tree to 30' by 1' dia. Drooping yellow twigs.
Lance-shaped leaves, green above to white below,
about 5" by 1". (4) Light straw with blackish
streaks. Works well.

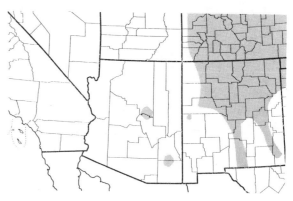

Peachleaf willow

WRIGHTS PEACHLEAF. (2) So. N.M., W Texas.
(3) Small tree. Leaves narrower than above; long
pointed at tip, short pointed at base. (4) Similar to
peachleaf.

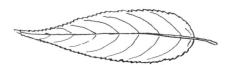

Wright's peachleaf willow

RED. (2) Not in N.M.; Ariz.-Huachuca Mts. northwest to Grand Canyon and Utah. (3) Small tree to
40' by 2'. Lance leaves to 6" by 1½". Twigs yellow
to brownish. Bark furrowed, dark brown. (4) Whitish sapwood; light reddish brown heart; brittle.

RYDBERG. (2) Listed from Capital Reef Nat'l.
Monument and in So. Utah. (3) Not known. (4) Not
known.

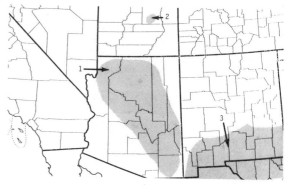

1. Red willow
2. Rydberg willow
3. Wright's peachleaf willow

SANDBAR. (2) Southeast border N.M. (3) Slender upright shrub or small tree to 30'. Leaves to 6" by 1/3"; margin toothed. Twigs green to brown. (4) Sapwood pale brown, heartwood reddish brown.

SUMMIT. (2) 10,500 to 12,500 ft. on highest mts. N.M. and near Springerville, Ariz. (3) Low prostrate shrub to 6" high. Small leaves about 1" by ½" clustered at branch ends. Stems often root on ground contact. (4) Too small.

WHIPLASH. (2) Ponderosa pine forest near Santa Fe, N.M. and near Springerville, Ariz. (3) Tall slender shrub. Leaves about 3" by 1", long pointed. Bright yellow to orange twigs. (4) Not known. Too small to use.

YELLOW. (2) White Mts. and No. N.M., NE Ariz. (3) Shrubs only. Twigs yellow. Leaves lance-shaped to 3" long, short pointed, rounded at base. (4) Too small to use.

YEWLEAF ("Tarais"). (2) Extreme s.w. N.M. and s.e. Ariz. and w. Texas. (3) Small tree to 40' by 2'. Twigs densely white or silver haired at first. Very small, narrow, crowded leaves about 1" by ½". (4) Sapwood white; heartwood dark brown.

Map combined with Arroyo willow

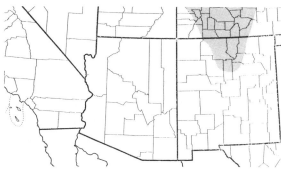

Summit willow

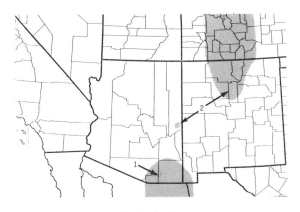

1. Yewleaf willow
2. Whiplash willow

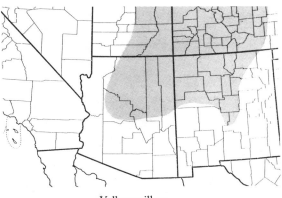

Yellow willow

Yewleaf willow

163

GLOSSARY

ALTERNATE— Scattered singly along the axis.

AWL-SHAPED—Tapering from the base to a slender point.

AXIL—Upper angle formed by a leaf or branch with the stem.

BRACT—A modified leaf-form subtending a flower.

COROLLA—The inner part of the perianth (which see), made up of petals.

DENTATE—Toothed, with teeth pointed outward.

GLABROUS—Not hairy, smooth.

HIRSUTE—Hairy.

INVOLUCRE—A circle of bracts around a cluster of flowers.

LEAFLET—A small blade of a compound leaf.

PINNATE—A compound leaf with leaflets along each side of a footstalk.

RACHIS—An axis bearing leaflets or flowers.

TERMINAL—At the end of a branch.

WING—A thin and dry extension of an organ.

WOOLLY—Having a cover of long, tangled hairs.

Flowers, Trees and Ferns of Anza-Borrego Desert State Park, 1965

Aztec Ruins National Monument, Native Trees and Shrubs, N.P.S.

Trees and Shrubs of Bandelier National Monument

Master Plan, Bryce Canyon National Park (trees and shrubs),
        Richard W. Russell, 1965

Plant Check List, Canyon de Chelly National Monument

*Resources Management Plan, Canyonlands National Park, Arches and
        Natural Bridges National Monuments*

A Checklist of the Plants of Capitol Reef Area, Ralph C. Webb, 1967

Checklist of the Flora of Capulin Mountain National Monument,
        Craig B. Jones, 1970

*Vascular Plants of Carlsbad Caverns National Park, New Mexico and
        Adjacent Guadalupe Mountains*, 1969

Woody Plants of Cedar Breaks National Monument, William H. Ehorn

*Checklist and Descriptions of the Trees and Shrubs in Chiricahua National
        Monument*

*Common Trees and Shrubs Occurring within the Memorial, Coronado
        National Memorial*

El Morro National Monument Trees and Shrubs

Personal correspondence, Fort Union National Monument

Checklist of Plants of Ganado, Linlichee, Nazlini, Elizabeth Young and
        Betty Anderson

*Common Shrubs and Vines, and Trees at Gila Cliff Dwellings National
        Monument*

Notes on the Human Ecology of Glenn Canyon, Angus M. Woodbury, 1965

Plant Checklist, Grand Canyon National Park, Pauline Mead Patraw

Checklist of Plants of Joshua Tree National Monument, Charles F. Adams 1957

Annotated Checklist of the Plants of Mesa Verde, Colorado, Stanley L. Welsh
        and James A. Erdman, 1964

*Complete list of the plants in the herbarium at Montezuma Castle National
        Monument*, 1964

A checklist of the Plants of Organ Pipe National Monument, Burnette Adams,
        1971

Plants of Pecos National Monument, Pauline M. Patraw

A Checklist of Plants of Petrified Forest National Park, Larry Henderson

Plant List for Saguaro National Monument, Richard Wadleigh, 1969

A Checklist of the Vascular Flora of Tonto National Monument, Arizona,
    Robert L. Burgess, 1965

List of Plants of Walnut Canyon

Plants and Animals of White Sands, N.P.S., 1969

Seed Plants of Wupatki and Sunset Crater National Monuments,
    W. B. McDougall, 1962

Common Plant Checklist of Zion National Park

Check List of Native Vegetation in the Southwestern Region, Forest Service,
    Department of Agriculture, 1963

Arnberger, Leslie P. 1952. *Flowers of the Southwest Mountains.*
Southwestern Monuments Association, Globe, Arizona. Popular
Series no. 7, 112 pp., illus.

Benson, Lyman. 1950. *The Cacti of Arizona.* University of Arizona, 2d edition.

Benson, Lyman, and Robert A. Darrow. 1945. *A Manual of Southwestern
Desert Trees and Shrubs.* University of Arizona Press, Tucson. Biol.
Bul. No. 6, 411 pp., illus.

Dodge, Natt N. 1954. *Flowers of the Southwest Deserts.* Southwestern
Monuments Association, Globe, Arizona. Popular series no. 4,
112 pp., illus.

Featherly, Henry Ira. 1954. *Taxonomic Terminology of the Higher Plants.*
Iowa State College Press, Ames. 166 pp.

Forest Service, Department of Agriculture. 1937. *Range Plant Handbook,*
U. S. Government Printing Office.

Goodding, Leslie N. 1938. *Notes on Native and Exotic Plants in Region
Eight, with Specific Reference to Their Value in the Soil Conservation
Program.* U.S.D.A., Soil Conservation Service, Region Eight,
Albuquerque, N.M. 152 pp., illus.

Harlow, William M., and Ellwood S. Harrar. 1950. *Textbook of Dendrology.*
McGraw-Hill Book Co., New York. 3rd ed., 555 pp., illus.

Harrington, Harold D. 1954. *Manual of the Plants of Colorado.* Sage
Books, Denver. x + 666 pp.

Kearney, Thomas H., and Robert H. Peebles and collaborators. 1951.
Arizona Flora. University of California Press, Berkeley. 1032 pp.

Kelley, George W. *A Guide to the Woody Plants of Colorado.* Pruett
Publishing Company, Boulder, Colorado. 180 pp., illus.

Kelsey, Harlan P., and William A. Dayton. 1942. *Standardized Plant Names.*
J. Horace McFarland Co., Harrisburg, Pa. 2nd ed., 675 pp.

Lamb, Samuel H. 1971. *Woody Plants of New Mexico and Their Value to
Wildlife.* New Mexico Department of Game and Fish, Santa Fe,
New Mexico, Bulletin No. 14, 80 pp., illus.

Little, Elbert L., Jr. 1950. *Southwestern Trees: A Guide to the Native
Species of New Mexico and Arizona.* U. S. Government Printing
Office, Washington, D. C. Agric. Handbook No. 9, 109 pp., illus.

1953. *Checklist of Native and Naturalized Trees of the United
States (Including Alaska).* U. S. Govt. Printing Office, Washington, D.C.
Agric. Handbook No. 41, 472 pp.

Longyear, Burton O. 1927. *Trees and Shrubs of the Rocky Mountain Region.*
G. P. Putnam's Sons, New York. 244 pp., illus.

Lowe, Charles H. 1964. *The Vertebrates of Arizona.* The University of Arizona Press, Tucson. 270 pp., illus.

Mirov, N.T. 1968. *The Genus Pinus.* Ronald Press, New York. 602 pp., illus.

Patraw, Pauline M. 1951. *Flowers of the Southwest Mesas.* Southwestern Monuments Association, Globe, Arizona. 112 pp., illus.

Pesman, M. Walter. 1962. *Meet Flora Mexicana.* Dale Stuart King, Publisher, Globe, Arizona. 278 pp., illus.

Preston, Richard J., Jr. 1947. *Rocky Mountain Trees.* Iowa State College Press, Ames. 2nd ed., 285 pp., illus.

Sargent, Charles Sprague. 1926. *Manual of the Trees of North America.* Houghton-Mifflin Co., Boston. 2nd ed., 910 pp., illus.

Standley, Paul C. 1920-1923. *Trees and Shrubs of Mexico.* Contrib. United States Herbarium, Vol. 23. Smithsonian Press, Washington, D. C. 1721 pp.

U.S. Dept. of Agriculture. 1949. *Trees.* The Yearbook of Agriculture. U.S. Govt. Printing Office, Washington, D.C. xiv+944 pp., illus.

Vines, Robert A. 1960. *Trees, Shrubs and Woody Vines of the Southwest.* University of Texas Press, Austin. xii + 1104 pp., illus.

Wooton, E. O., and Paul C. Standley. 1915. *The Flora of New Mexico.*

NOTES